W9-ARQ-692

DANGEROUS Prayers

50 POWERFUL PRAYERS THAT CHANGED THE WORLD

Portrait Illustrations by Francesca Resta

Additional Illustrations by Isabella Grott and Julianne St. Clair

THOMAS NELSON

Since 1798

© 2019 Thomas Nelson

All rights reserved. No portion of this book may be reproduced, stored in a retrieval system, or transmitted in any form or by any means—electronic, mechanical, photocopy, recording, scanning, or other—except for brief quotations in critical reviews or articles, without the prior written permission of the publisher.

Published in Nashville, Tennessee, by Thomas Nelson. Thomas Nelson is a registered trademark of HarperCollins Christian Publishing, Inc.

Compiled by Susan Hill

Portrait illustrations by Francesca Resta

Additional illustrations by Isabella Grott and Julianne St. Clair

Thomas Nelson titles may be purchased in bulk for educational, business, fund-raising, or sales promotional use. For information, please e-mail SpecialMarkets@ThomasNelson.com.

Unless otherwise noted, Scripture quotations are taken from the New King James Version®. © 1982 by Thomas Nelson. Used by permission. All rights reserved.

Scripture quotations marked NIV are from the Holy Bible, New International Version®, NIV®. Copyright © 1973, 1978, 1984, 2011 by Biblica, Inc.® Used by permission of Zondervan. All rights reserved worldwide. www.Zondervan.com. The "NIV" and "New International Version" are trademarks registered in the United States Patent and Trademark Office by Biblica, Inc.®

Any Internet addresses, phone numbers, or company or product information printed in this book are offered as a resource and are not intended in any way to be or to imply an endorsement by Thomas Nelson, nor does Thomas Nelson vouch for the existence, content, or services of these sites, phone numbers, companies, or products beyond the life of this book.

ISBN 978-1-4002-0905-7

Printed in China

19 20 21 22 23   HaHa   10 9 8 7 6 5 4 3 2 1

CONTENTS

RICHARD ALLEN

(1760–1831)

R ichard Allen is widely recognized as the denominational founder of the African Methodist Episcopal (AME) Church, the first independent black denomination.

Allen was born into slavery in Philadelphia in 1760. He became a Christian when he was seventeen and began preaching on his plantation and at local Methodist churches whenever he had the opportunity. In time, his master became a Christian and allowed Allen to purchase his freedom.

In 1781, Allen began circuit preaching in Delaware and the surrounding states. Five years later, he returned to Philadelphia and became a member at St. George's Methodist Church. His leadership attracted other African Americans to the church, and racial tensions escalated. In 1786, white and black people often worshipped together, but blacks were forced into segregated seating and inconvenient service times.

Allen realized the African American community needed its own house

of worship. Though he had no desire to leave the Methodist Church, and although denominational leaders resisted, he founded the Bethel African Methodist Episcopal Church. Bishop Francis Asbury dedicated the building and ordained Allen as a deacon.

Despite attempts by white Methodist leaders to keep Allen's congregation and property under their jurisdiction, in 1816, the Pennsylvania Supreme Court ruled the church belonged to Allen and his congregants. Later that year, the AME became a recognized denomination, and Allen was ordained as an elder and bishop, becoming the first African American to hold the office in the United States. The denomination grew rapidly and today has more than two million members.

O, precious blood of my dear Redeemer! O, gaping wounds of my crucified Savior! Who can contemplate the sufferings of God incarnate, and not raise his hope, and not put his trust in Him? What, though my body be crumbled into dust, and that dust blown over the face of the earth, yet I undoubtedly know my Redeemer lives, and shall raise me up at the last day; whether I am comforted or left desolate; whether I enjoy peace or am afflicted with temptations; whether I am healthful or sickly, succored or abandoned by the good things of this life, I will always hope in Thee, O, my chiefest, infinite good.

—RICHARD ALLEN

AUGUSTINE OF HIPPO

(354–430)

Augustine was an early Christian theologian and philosopher whose writings impacted the development of Western Christianity and philosophy. Augustine was an unlikely scholar. At age seventeen, when he left his small North African town for school in Carthage, he was considered an underachiever who was more interested in wayward living than schoolwork. But Augustine threw himself into his studies and became known for his intellectual curiosity. By the time he completed his studies, he'd forsaken his mother's Christian faith, although she continued to pray for his conversion.

After teaching for a season, Augustine entered a time of personal struggle and a shift in philosophies. He was wrestling with the concept of personal sin when he read the writing of the apostle Paul in Romans 13:13–14. Augustine later wrote, "No further would I read; nor needed I: for instantly at the end of this sentence, by a light as it were of serenity infused into my heart, all the darkness of doubt vanished away."

Following his conversion, Augustine resigned from his professorship. In 391, Augustine arrived in Hippo, intending to set up a monastery. Instead, against his desire, he was made a priest. Five years later, he became the bishop of Hippo.

Augustine was tasked with the job of defending Christianity against allegations that it had caused the Roman Empire's downfall by shifting eyes away from Roman gods. Augustine's response to the criticism came in a body of written work. His most important writings are *The City of God*, *On Christian Doctrine*, and *Confessions*. Augustine died from fever at age seventy-six, but his work survived, and his theology became foundational as the early church was built.

Listen to my supplication, Master, so that my soul doesn't stagger under Your instruction, so that I don't stumble in testifying to Your mercies, by which You tore me away from all my ruinous pathways. Thus You'll grow sweet to me beyond all that led me wrong, in my willingness to follow it. Thus I'll love You most mightily, and grasp Your hand with all the strength of my inmost being. Thus You'll tear me away from every trial, clear to the end.

—Augustine, based on 1 Corinthians 1:8

JOHANN SEBASTIAN BACH

(1685–1750)

Bach was born in Eisenach, Thuringia (Germany), into a family that produced fifty-three notable musicians in seven generations. Bach received his first music lessons from his father, Johann Ambrosius, a town musician, but by age ten, Bach was an orphan and went to live and study music with his older brother, Johann Christoph. Early on, it was apparent that Bach possessed extraordinary talent.

In 1723, after years of study and having held several prominent musical positions, Bach settled in Leipzig, Germany, where he remained until his death. He became the musical director and choirmaster of St. Thomas church and school. Bach's tenure there was dismal. He struggled with the town council, who was critical of his work and unwilling to pay him a reasonable salary. Yet, it was in this unfortunate environment that Bach wrote his most enduring music, including his classic *Mass in B Minor*, *The Passion of St. John*, and *The Passion of St. Matthew*.

Today a composer who writes one cantata a year is highly esteemed. For a season, Back was writing a cantata every week, 202 of which remain. Johann knew that without Jesus' help, he would never be able to complete the task of composing each new piece, so before writing the first note, Johann carefully wrote the letters *J J*—short for *Jesu, Juva,* or "Jesus, Help"—at the top of the page. With that, the music began to pour from his soul and onto the page. When he was finally satisfied, he wrote the letters *SDG* at the bottom of the page. These letters stood for *Soli Deo Gloria*—"for the glory of God alone." His prayer was that whenever the music was played, it would point toward God.

Nearly 75 percent of Bach's one thousand compositions were written for use in worship. Because of his talent, his love for Christ, and the impact of his musical contributions, Bach is often called "the Fifth Evangelist."

Jesus, help me show
Your glory through
the music I write.
May it bring You joy
even as it brings joy
to Your people.

—Johann Sebastian Bach

MARY MCLEOD BETHUNE

(1875–1955)

—✦—

Mary McLeod Bethune, an educational pioneer and a champion of racial and gender equality, was born on July 10, 1875, one of the youngest of the seventeen children of former slaves Samuel and Patsy McLeod. Following the Civil War, her mother continued working for her former owner until she saved enough money to purchase the land on which the McLeod family would grow cotton.

Bethune benefited from postwar efforts to educate African Americans, graduating from Scotia Seminary boarding school in 1894. She went on to attend Dwight Moody's Institute for Home and Foreign Missions in Chicago and became an educator. While teaching in South Carolina, she met and married fellow teacher Albertus Bethune, and they had a son in 1899.

In 1904, Bethune opened the Daytona Beach Literary and Industrial School for Training Negro Girls, a boarding school. The school later merged with the Cookman Institute and became Bethune-Cookman College in

1929. Bethune was a tireless advocate for gender and racial equality and went on to become the highest-ranking African American woman in government when she was named director of Negro Affairs of the National Youth Administration by President Franklin Roosevelt.

In 1940, she became vice president of the National Association for the Advancement of Colored People (NAACP). Bethune was also a member of the advisory board that created the Women's Army Corps in 1942. In 1945, she was appointed by President Harry S. Truman to serve as the only woman of color at the founding conference for the United Nations. Bethune's life was celebrated with a variety of awards, including a memorial statue in Washington, DC, and a postage stamp was issued in her honor in 1985. Today her final home is recognized as a National Historic Site.

Father, we call Thee Father because we love Thee. We are glad to be called Thy children, and to dedicate our lives to the service that extends through willing hearts and hands to the betterment of all mankind. . . . Grant us strength and courage and faith and humility sufficient for the tasks assigned to us.

—MARY MCLEOD BETHUNE

DIETRICH BONHOEFFER

(1906–1945)

❧————————————————————☙

Dietrich Bonhoeffer was a German pastor, theologian, and author known for his resistance to Adolf Hitler and the Nazi regime. He was among a small number of dissidents who worked from the inside to dismantle the Third Reich.

Bonhoeffer, a young pastor and speaker when Hitler rose to power, was one of the earliest critics of the Nazi regime. He was among a group of pastors and theologians who launched the Confessing Church, a movement that denounced the infiltration of Nazi ideology in the German Evangelical Church.

During his short lifetime, Bonhoeffer wrote a number of books, including the Christian classics *The Cost of Discipleship* and *Life Together.* He also pastored several congregations and trained young ministers.

Because of Bonhoeffer's outspoken political opinions, he eventually became a person of interest to the Nazi regime. Ultimately, Bonhoeffer was

charged with his connections to resistance groups, and he was arrested and taken to a concentration camp, where he spent two years before being sentenced to death. He was executed shortly before the end of the World War II.

A decade after Bonhoeffer's death, a doctor who was present at his murder described Bonhoeffer's last moments:

> The prisoners . . . were taken from their cells, and the verdicts of court-martial read out to them. Through the half-open door in one room of the huts, I saw Pastor Bonhoeffer, before taking off his prison garb, kneeling on the floor praying fervently to his God. I was most deeply moved by the way this lovable man prayed, so devout and so certain that God heard his prayer. At the place of execution, he again said a prayer and then climbed the steps to the gallows, brave and composed. His death ensued in a few seconds. In the almost fifty years that I have worked as a doctor, I have hardly ever seen a man die so entirely submissive to the will of God.

Restore me to liberty,

and enable me so to live now

that I may answer before Thee and

before the world.

Lord, whatever this day may bring,

Thy Name be praised.

Amen.

—DIETRICH BONHOEFFER,
WRITTEN WHILE AWAITING EXECUTION
IN A NAZI CONCENTRATION CAMP

CORRIE TEN BOOM

(1892–1983)

❧ ——————————————————— ❧

On April 15, 1892, Corrie ten Boom was the youngest of four children born to a Christian family in Haarlem, Netherlands. The early years of her life were spent peacefully living above her family's watch shop in her hometown. But when World War II began, the ten Booms felt compelled to help the Jews who were being pursued by the Nazis. They built a secret room behind a false wall in Corrie's bedroom that could hold up to six people. Corrie and her family assisted an estimated eight hundred people fleeing from the Gestapo.

On February 28, 1944, an informant posing as a refugee betrayed the ten Booms. Corrie and her family were arrested and put in prison. Her eighty-four-year-old father died after only a few days in custody. During the next ten months, Corrie and her sister, Betsie, were sent to three different prisons, the last being the notorious Ravensbrück concentration camp. While in prison, Corrie and Betsie shared the gospel and led worship services using a Bible they had smuggled into the camp. Betsie did not survive Ravensbrück.

Shortly after Betsie's death, Corrie was released due to an administrative error just one week before an order came to kill all the women her age.

Following the war, ten Boom traveled to more than sixty countries, sharing the message of the gospel and God's forgiveness. At one speaking event, she was confronted by a former guard from Ravensbrück who had been particularly cruel. The man had since become a Christian and had come to ask for her forgiveness, which she granted.

Ten Boom consistently shared a message of hope with her audiences, stating, "We have nothing to fear because Jesus is Victor, and He will never let us down. With Jesus, even in our darkest moments, the best remains. And the very best is yet to be."

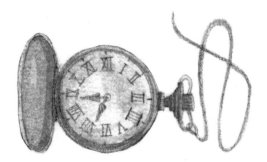

Jesus, help me!

I can lift my hand.

I can do that much.

You supply the feeling.

—Corrie ten Boom, on forgiving a Nazi
guard who worked at the concentration
camp where her sister was killed

EVANGELINE CORY BOOTH

(1865–1950)

Evangeline Cory Booth was born in London to William and Catherine Booth, founders of the Salvation Army, in 1865, the same year the Salvation Army was founded. She was named after Eva St. Claire, a Christian heroine in the novel *Uncle Tom's Cabin.*

Booth began preaching when she was fifteen and demonstrated her parents' same passion for ministry. Within two years she was given her own ministry post and quickly earned the nickname "White Angel of the Slums."

Booth's leadership skills were apparent early on, and she was known for both her problem solving and her proven ability to communicate the Salvation Army's cause. When trouble occurred at a local branch or persecution erupted, it was Evangeline whom General William Booth sent to address the problem. When the organization's American leadership disagreed with her father and ultimately split to become the Volunteers of America, he sent Evangeline to resolve the organizational issues.

In 1934, Booth became general of the Salvation Army, and she held the position for five years. During her travels, she gave lectures that were eventually gathered into a volume titled *Toward a Better World.* Her writing included a catalog of hymns, her most famous being "The World for God." She once said, "It is not how many years we live, but rather what we do with them."

Booth died of arteriosclerosis on June 17, 1950, at the age of eight-five.

The world for God! The world for God!

There's nothing else will meet the hunger of

my soul.

I see forsaken children, I see the tears that fall

From women's eyes once merry, now never

laugh at all;

I see the sins and sorrows of those who sit in

darkness;

I see in lands far distant, the hungry and

oppressed.

But behold! On a hill, Calvary! Calvary!

—Evangeline Cory Booth

E. M. BOUNDS

(1835–1913)

Edward McKendree Bounds was known as a man of prayer. Bounds was born on August 15, 1835, in a small town in Missouri. He attended a one-room schoolhouse in Shelbyville, where his father worked as a county clerk. In the 1850s, Bounds studied law in Hannibal, Missouri. He was a studious young man and was admitted to the bar shortly before his nineteenth birthday. He was also committed to studying the Scriptures and was a student of John Wesley's sermons. He practiced law until he was twenty-four, when he felt called to full-time ministry.

In 1861, Bounds was serving as pastor of a Methodist Episcopal church when he was arrested by Union troops and charged with sympathizing with the Confederacy. He was made a prisoner of war and kept in custody for eighteen months before being transferred to Memphis, Tennessee, and finally released. Though he did not endorse slavery, Bounds traveled nearly one hundred miles on foot to join General Pierce's command in Mississippi.

Shortly after, he became the chaplain to the Confederate troops in Missouri. After John Hood's forces were defeated in Nashville, Tennessee, Bounds was captured once again and held until he swore loyalty to the United States.

Following the war, Bounds married Emma Barnett and fathered three children. He pastored a number of churches and spent the final years of his life reading, writing, and praying. Bounds routinely awoke at four each morning to pray. He believed prayer to be the most powerful link between man and God, and he authored numerous books on the subject of prayer. At the time of his death in August 1913, only two of his titles had been published, and he was still mostly unknown. Yet to date, no one has left a more significant inheritance of research into the discipline of prayer.

Lord, in the strength of grace,

With a glad heart and free,

Myself, my residue of days,

I consecrate to Thee.

Thy ransomed servant, I

Restore to Thee Thy own;

And from this moment, live or die,

To serve my God alone.

—E. M. Bounds

JOHN CALVIN

(1509–1564)

———————————

John Calvin is considered among the most influential Protestant theologians in Christian history. He is known as a reformer, a theologian, a teacher, and a church statesman.

While studying at the University of Orléans in France, Calvin was introduced to the early reform ideology of Martin Luther. He converted to Christianity and ultimately became the most influential figure in the second generation of the Protestant Reformation.

At twenty-five, just one year after his conversion, Calvin set to work writing what would become his landmark work, *Institutes of the Christian Religion*, in which he outlined the fundamentals of the Protestant faith. The book was published in 1536. Calvin's work emphasized the authority of the Bible and made a case for the Reformed views for the interpretation of Scripture.

Calvin briefly made his home in Geneva, Switzerland, where he pastored until 1538, when he refused to serve Communion to prominent but openly sinful members of his congregation. The resulting conflict was so great that he was forced to leave the city. He returned to Germany but was invited back to Geneva in 1541, where he became both a spiritual and political leader. Calvin utilized Protestant principles to establish a religious government. Under Calvin's leadership, Geneva became the center of Protestantism and the place where pastors were equipped and sent to the rest of Europe. Missionaries trained in Geneva were sent to Italy, Hungary, Poland, Germany, the Netherlands, England, Scotland, and Brazil.

Calvin's writings were extensive, and by the time of his death, he had written many of the foundational documents for the Reformed church as well as numerous books and Bible commentaries. Calvin died on May 27, 1564, and his last words were, "How long, O Lord?" from Psalm 79:5. He died quoting the Scriptures he had dedicated his life to preaching.

Grant, Almighty God, that as Thou shinest on us by Thy Word, we may not be blind at midday, nor willfully seek darkness, and thus lull our minds asleep, but that exercising ourselves in Thy Word, we may stir up ourselves more and more to fear Thy name, and thus present ourselves and all our pursuits, as a sacrifice to Thee, that Thou mayest peaceably rule and perpetually dwell in us, until Thou gatherest us to Thy celestial habitation, where there is reserved for us eternal rest and glory, through Jesus Christ our Lord. Amen.

—John Calvin

AMY CARMICHAEL

(1867–1951)

In 1867, Amy Carmichael was born the oldest of seven children in Belfast, Ireland, to a family of Scottish descent. After her father's death when she was eighteen, she lived with the family of Robert Wilson, who supported many missionaries around the world.

While in her twenties, Carmichael felt the call to missions. In November 1895, she volunteered with the Church of England Zenana Missionary Society and traveled to South India, where she would serve for the rest of her life.

Carmichael shared the gospel with the Indian women, and she soon found herself in charge of caring for the new converts. As she served the women, she learned that Indian parents commonly dedicated their children to the gods. As temple children, these youngsters were vulnerable to prostitution and other dangers. Carmichael made it her life's mission to rescue and care for these children. In 1927, she founded the Dohnavur

Fellowship to care for at-risk children. The orphanage relied on volunteers and financial support, although money was never solicited. Carmichael was the director, and the work done there became well-known through her writing.

In 1931, Carmichael suffered a fall that would impact her health and permanently restrict her movement. Even so, she went on to publish more than forty books.

Carmichael's long ministry in South India was fueled by the Scriptures and prayer. Carmichael died at Dohnavur in 1951. The word *Ammai*, meaning "revered mother," is inscribed on her gravestone. Work at the Dohnavur Fellowship continues today.

Holy Spirit,

think through me

till Your ideas

are my ideas.

—Amy Carmichael

GEORGE WASHINGTON CARVER

(ca.1864–1943)

George Washington Carver was one of the most prominent scientists and inventors of his time. Born into slavery in Diamond, Missouri, around 1864, he was the son of Mary and Giles, a slave couple owned by Moses Carver. Just one week after George's birth, slave raiders kidnapped him, his sister, and his mother and sold them in Kentucky. An agent of Moses Carver was sent to locate the family, but he was only able to find the infant George.

The end of the Civil War in 1865 ushered in the end of slavery in Missouri, but Moses and his wife, Susan, decided they would keep George and his brother, James, and raise them. No local school would accept the boys, so Susan educated them at home.

A quest for knowledge became a driving force in Carver's life. Carver began his botanical studies while he was a college student at Iowa State. After graduation, he embarked on a career in teaching and research. In

1896, Booker T. Washington, the principal of the African American Tuskegee Institute, hired Carver to lead the school's agricultural department.

Carver became known for inventing more than one hundred products, including plastics, dyes, and gasoline—all from the peanut plant. He went on to receive national acclaim for his work, and President Theodore Roosevelt sought Carver's counsel on agricultural matters. Carver used his celebrity status to promote scientific causes until the end of his life. He died in 1943 after a fall in his home. His epitaph reads, "He could have added fortune to fame, but caring for neither, he found happiness and honor in being helpful to the world."

O God, I thank Thee
for such a direct
manifestation of Thy
goodness, majesty,
and power.

—George Washington Carver

OSWALD CHAMBERS

(1874–1917)

Before being catapulted into full-time Christian ministry, twenty-two-year-old Oswald Chambers wrote, "I feel I shall be buried for a time, hidden away in obscurity; then suddenly I shall flame out, do my work, and be gone." At the time he wrote those words, Chambers had no idea that after only fifteen years of ministry, he would die suddenly at age forty-three. But following death, his ministry was far from over. Chambers's classic devotional, *My Utmost for His Highest*, which was published posthumously along with more than fifty other devotionals he authored, remains one of the most widely read devotionals ever written.

Chambers was born the son of a Baptist preacher in Aberdeen, Scotland. He became a Christian because of the preaching of Charles Spurgeon. After a time of spiritual desperation during his college years, Chambers trusted in Jesus' promise that God would give the Spirit to those who ask, freeing him from fears about his own immorality and weak faith.

Chambers became a powerful speaker, and soon he had an increasingly busy speaking and teaching ministry, taking him to the United States and Japan. During the last six years of Chambers's life, he ran London's Bible Training College, which he had opened in 1911, and served as chaplain to the British Commonwealth troops in Egypt during World War I.

In 1917, Chambers suffered complications from a ruptured appendix, and he died suddenly. Following his death, Chambers's wife transcribed and published his sermons and lectures as pamphlets. Eventually she gathered the lectures in book form and published them in 1927—as *My Utmost for His Highest*.

How helpless I am in bringing
forth fruit, Thy kind of fruit
in the world, so ungenerous
and unlike Thee am I. Forgive
me, and by abiding in Jesus
may I bear much fruit and
so glorify the Father.

—Oswald Chambers

FANNY CROSBY

(1820–1915)

———✦———

Fanny Crosby penned more than nine thousand hymns, which is a remarkable feat for any writer, but even more impressive considering she was blind.

Crosby was born in Putnam County, New York. Before she was two months old, she fell ill. Regrettably, the family doctor was out of town, and a man posing as a physician applied hot mustard plaster to her eyes, leaving her permanently blind. Shortly after, her father died. Crosby's mother went to work as a maid to support the family, and Fanny was mostly raised by her grandmother.

As a young girl, Crosby enjoyed poetry and was passionate about memorizing the Scriptures. She memorized five chapters a week and could recite the Pentateuch, the Gospels, Proverbs, Song of Solomon, and numerous psalms from memory while still a child. By the time she turned fifteen, she was admitted to the New York Institute for the Blind. She would spend the

next twenty-three years there, the first twelve as a student and the remainder as a teacher.

In 1858, Crosby married Alexander van Alstine, a former student at the institute. Alstine was considered to be among New York's finest organists, and he and Crosby collaborated on hymns, with her writing the lyrics and him providing the melody. Crosby was under contract with her publisher to turn in three hymns each week but often wrote up to six or seven a day. Ultimately, her hymns would be included in the hymnals of every denomination in the Christian faith.

Crosby never considered her blindness as an obstacle. She said, "Do you know that if at birth I had been able to make one petition, it would have been that I was born blind? Because when I get to heaven, the first face that shall ever gladden my sight will be that of my Savior."

I am praying, blessed Savior,
To be more and more like Thee;
I am praying that Thy Spirit
Like a dove may rest on me.

Thou who knowest all my weakness,
Thou who knowest all my care,
While I plead each precious promise,
Hear, oh hear, and answer prayer.

I am praying to be humbled
By the power of grace divine,
To be clothed upon with meekness,
And to have no will but Thine.

—Fanny Crosby

THOMAS DORSEY

(1899–1993)

❧ ————————————————————— ❧

Thomas Dorsey is known as the father of gospel music. Dorsey was born in Georgia, the son of a Baptist preacher and a church organist. As a child, Dorsey felt torn between sacred and secular music. He left school at age eleven to work in a vaudeville theater. Six years later, he moved from Atlanta to Chicago and found immediate success as a piano player in the Windy City.

Under the name "Georgia Tom," Dorsey performed with blues artist Ma Rainey and her Wild Cats Jazz Band. But his hectic, after-hours lifestyle eventually led to a nervous breakdown, and he went home to Georgia to recuperate. His mother pleaded with him to quit playing blues and to commit himself instead to sacred music, but he ignored her and returned to Chicago, getting married there and continuing his gig with Ma Rainey. Soon a second breakdown left Dorsey unable to play music for a season.

Dorsey's life unraveled in August 1932, when his wife and son died during childbirth. In his grief, he turned to the piano for comfort, writing his

now-famous hymn "Precious Lord, Take My Hand," which he said came directly from God. Dorsey wrote more than four hundred compositions during his lifetime, but it is for this song that he is best known.

In 1933, Dorsey founded the National Convention of Gospel Choirs and Choruses. Six years later, he partnered with Mahalia Jackson, and the pair ushered in what we now refer to as the "Golden Age of Gospel Music." Dorsey died in 1993.

Precious Lord, take my hand,

lead me on, let me stand,

I am tired, I am weak, I am worn;

Through the storm, through the night,

lead me on to the light:

Take my hand, precious Lord, lead me home.

—Thomas Dorsey, "Precious Lord, Take My
Hand," *The United Methodist Hymnal*, no. 474

FREDERICK DOUGLASS

(ca. 1818–1895)

Frederick Douglass was a prominent nineteenth-century writer and speaker in the antislavery movement. Born into slavery sometime around 1818, Douglass was never sure of his exact date of birth. As an infant, he was separated from his mother and lived for a time with his maternal grandmother. When he was six years old, he was taken from his grandmother and sent to work on the Wye House plantation in Maryland.

During his time as a slave, Douglass learned to read and write. By the time he was sent to work for William Freeland, he was using the Bible to teach other slaves to read. Word got out, and Douglass, at sixteen, was sent to work for farmer Edward Covey, a man known for his brutality. In 1838, after several failed attempts, Douglass escaped Covey's farm. He married Anna Murray, and they had five children together.

The couple moved to Massachusetts, and Douglass began attending meetings of the abolitionist movement. He soon became a speaker and

leader in the campaign for human rights. Douglass would publish five autobiographies, including his well-known *Narrative of the Life of Frederick Douglass, an American Slave*. He traveled domestically and internationally as a speaker, and in 1847, he began publishing his own abolition newsletter, *The North Star.*

Until his death in 1895, Douglass remained an active speaker, writer, and human rights activist. He died after suffering a heart attack as he traveled home from a meeting of the fledgling, Washington, DC–based National Council of Women. His legacy still inspires those who seek a more equitable world.

You are loosed from your moorings, and are free; I am fast in my chains and am a slave! You move merrily before the gentle gale, and I sadly before the bloody whip! You are freedom's swift-winged angels, that fly round the world; I am confined in bands of iron! O that I were free! O, that I were on one of Your gallant decks, and under Your protecting wing! Alas! betwixt me and You, the turbid waters roll. Go on, go on. O that I could also go! Could I but swim! If I could fly! O, why was I born a man, of whom to make a brute! The glad ship is gone; she hides in the dim distance. I am left in the hottest hell of unending slavery. O God, save me! God, deliver me! . . . I have only one life to lose. I had as well be killed running as die standing. Only think of it; one hundred miles straight north, and I am free! Try it? Yes! God helping me, I will.

—FREDERICK DOUGLASS, A PRAYER FOR DELIVERANCE, WRITTEN DURING HIS ENSLAVEMENT

W. E. B. DU BOIS

(1868–1963)

W. E. B. Du Bois was an American civil rights activist, scholar, educator, writer, and poet. Du Bois was born February 23, 1868, in Great Barrington, Massachusetts. He married Nina Gomer, and they had two children together.

Du Bois was a gifted scholar and in 1895 became the first African American to receive a doctorate from Harvard University. He went on to serve as a professor at the University of Pennsylvania and at Atlanta University. Du Bois's contributions as a writer include novels, poetry, essays, as well as histories.

In 1909, Du Bois became one of the founding members of the National Association for the Advancement of Colored People (NAACP). From 1910 to 1934, he served as its director of publicity and research and as editor for its monthly magazine, *The Crisis*, which offered young African American

writers a platform to inform readers of civil rights, historical, political, and cultural issues.

Du Bois was also active on behalf of Pan-Africanism and was heavily involved in the efforts of people of African descent all over the world, even organizing a series of Pan-African congresses in various countries. In 1961, he moved to Ghana and worked as the director of Encyclopedia Africana, remaining in Ghana until his death on August 27, 1963. Du Bois was given a state funeral and deemed a "phenomenon" by the president of Ghana, Kwame Nkrumah.

Give us grace, O God, to dare to do the deed which we well know cries to be done. Let us not hesitate because of ease, or the words of men's mouths, or our own lives. Mighty causes are calling us—the freeing of women, the training of children, the putting down of hate and murder and poverty— all these and more. But they call with voices that mean work and sacrifice and death. Mercifully grant us, O God, the spirit of Esther, that we say: I will go unto the King and if I perish, I perish.

—W. E. B. Du Bois

JONATHAN EDWARDS

(1703–1758)

Jonathan Edwards is considered by many to be America's most significant theologian. Edwards was born in Connecticut and in 1722 earned his master's degree from Yale. After a two-year apprenticeship with his grandfather, he became the preacher at a church in Northampton, Massachusetts. It was during this time he met and married Sarah Pierrepont, and they eventually had eleven children.

In 1734, Edwards was preaching on justification by faith when a spiritual revival occurred. That December there were six conversions, and by the following spring, there was about thirty conversions each week. Edwards kept a written record of what he witnessed and published it in his 1737 work *A Faithful Narrative of the Surprising Work of God*. His most compelling sermons were published in 1738 in his *Justification by Faith*. Both volumes were widely read in America and England and served to fuel the Great Awakening a few years later when George Whitefield's preaching influenced thousands

of people to turn to Christ. In 1754, Edwards wrote *Freedom of the Will*, a defense of the sovereignty of God.

It was during the Great Awakening that Edwards preached "Sinners in the Hands of an Angry God," which many believe to be the most famous sermon in American history. Regrettably, the sermon has been used to portray Edwards as condemning and overly emotional when in reality he preached it impassively.

In 1758, the College of New Jersey, which would later be known as Princeton University, named Edwards president. Shortly after his arrival, he died at age fifty-five of complications from the smallpox vaccination, but his legacy has continued to impact Christians worldwide.

Lord, grant that from hence I may learn to withdraw my thoughts, affections, desires, and expectations entirely from the world, and may fix them upon the heavenly state, where there is fullness of joy; where reigns heavenly, sweet, calm, and delightful love without alloy, where there are continually the dearest expressions of this love; where there is the enjoyment of this love without ever parting; and where those persons who appear so lovely in this world, will be inexpressibly more lovely, and full of love to us.

—Jonathan Edwards

ELISABETH ELLIOT

(1926–2015)

Elisabeth Elliot is known as a missionary, an author, a speaker, and one of the most influential Christian women of the twentieth century. She was born Elisabeth Howard in Belgium, the daughter of missionaries. Her family moved to the United States when she was an infant.

After high school, Elisabeth studied classical Greek at Wheaton College. While there, she met Jim Elliot. Following graduation, and for five years before their engagement, the couple served in separate areas of Ecuador. In 1953, Jim and Elisabeth married in Quito, Ecuador, and continued their ministry.

Jim's goal was to enter the territory of an unreached people group, and he focused his attention on the Aucas, a violent tribe that no one had survived meeting. He and four other missionaries entered Auca territory and made friendly contact but were speared to death. Elisabeth was left a widow and the sole provider for their ten-month-old daughter.

In spite of the tragedy, Elliot remained in Ecuador and continued to minister to the Quichua tribe. Around the same time, she met two women from the Auca tribe who lived with her and taught her the Auca language. Afterward, she went as a missionary to evangelize the very tribe that had murdered her husband.

Elliot began her writing career in Ecuador and eventually wrote twenty-four books. In 1963, she returned to the United States and began a career as a speaker and radio host. For thirteen years, Elliot hosted a radio show for women called *Gateway to Joy*. In 1969, she married Addison Leitch, a professor of theology at Gordon Conwell Seminary in Massachusetts. They were married until his death in 1973. She married Lars Gren in 1977, and he cared for her during her decade-long battle with dementia and until her death in 2015.

Loving Lord and heavenly Father, I offer up today all that I am, all that I have, all that I do, and all that I suffer, to be Yours today and Yours forever. Give me grace, Lord, to do all that I know of Your holy will. Purify my heart, sanctify my thinking, correct my desires. Teach me, in all of today's work and trouble and joy, to respond with honest praise, simple trust, and instant obedience, that my life may be in truth a living sacrifice, by the power of Your Holy Spirit and in the name of Your Son Jesus Christ, my Master and my all. Amen.

—ELISABETH ELLIOT

FRANCIS OF ASSISI

(ca. 1181–1226)

❦ ──────────────────────────── ❦

Francis of Assisi was born Francesco di Pietro di Bernardone in Assisi, Italy, the son of a prosperous merchant. As a young man, he was carefree and frivolous, according to biographers. In 1202, he marched audaciously into the battle against the city of Perugia and was taken prisoner. He spent a year in captivity before his father could arrange ransom. After his release, he spent a transformative year recuperating in Assisi.

During his convalescence, Francis experienced numerous dreams and visions. Once, while praying in a rundown church in San Damiano, he said he heard Jesus say three times from the cross, "Francis, go repair my house, which, as you can see, is falling completely to ruin." Francis took that to mean that he was to repair the church in which he was praying, so he sold off family goods for repairs. As Francis continued to have these experiences, he came to believe he was called to live a simple, secluded life and preach a gospel of repentance.

By 1209, a group of twelve men who felt called to a similar life and ministry gathered around Francis. This band of men would become the First Order of Franciscans. Francis wrote a rule for the order and traveled to Rome to seek the church's approval for his work. His brothers, called friars, multiplied in number and were soon traveling the world, preaching a message of simplicity, repentance, and obedience to the teachings of Christ.

By Francis's midforties, he was in poor health and had lost his eyesight. Even so, in his final years, he wrote his famous *Canticle of Brother Sun*.

Contemporaries of Francis said he lived the Sermon on the Mount more consistently than anyone else except Jesus. His legacy continues to impact the world today.

Lord, make me an instrument of Your peace:

where there is hatred, let me sow love;

where there is injury, pardon;

where there is doubt, faith;

where there is despair, hope;

where there is darkness, light;

where there is sadness, joy.

O divine Master, grant that I may not so much seek

to be consoled as to console,

to be understood as to understand,

to be loved as to love.

For it is in giving that we receive,

it is in pardoning that we are pardoned,

and it is in dying that we are born to eternal life.

Amen.

—Francis of Assisi

BILLY GRAHAM

(1918–2018)

———

illy Graham has been called "the evangelist to the world" with good reason. During his ministry, this North Carolina native preached the gospel of Jesus Christ to an estimated 215 million people spanning six continents and more than 185 countries and territories. In June 2005, at his final crusade, Graham said, "I have one message: that Jesus Christ came, He died on a cross, He rose again, and He asked us to repent of our sins and receive Him by faith as Lord and Savior, and if we do, we have forgiveness of all of our sins."

Graham held his first official crusade in 1947, but it was a ministry event in Los Angeles, California, in 1949 that captivated the country's attention. Initially, the meetings were scheduled to run for three weeks, but as hundreds of thousands of people gathered to listen to Graham's preaching, the crusade lasted for eight weeks.

Graham was a voice for racial equality. In 1973, at a preaching engagement

in Johannesburg, South Africa, Graham said, "Christ belongs to all people. He belongs to the whole world. . . . I reject any creed based on hate. . . . Christianity is not a white man's religion, and don't let anybody ever tell you that it's white or black."

Preaching the gospel to the multitudes was Graham's primary goal, but he also served as a spiritual counselor to presidents and prayed with every US president from Harry S. Truman to Barack Obama. Graham is the author of thirty-four books and a recipient of the Congressional Gold Medal. Gallup listed him as one of the "Ten Most Admired Men" sixty-one times.

Our Father and our God, we praise You for Your goodness to our nation, giving us blessings far beyond what we deserve. Yet we know all is not right with America. We deeply need a moral and spiritual renewal to help us meet the many problems we face. Convict us of sin. Help us to turn to You in repentance and faith. Set our feet on the path of Your righteousness and peace. We pray today for our nation's leaders. Give them the wisdom to know what is right, and the courage to do it. You have said, "Blessed is the nation whose God is the Lord." May this be a new era for America, as we humble ourselves and acknowledge You alone as our Savior and Lord. This we pray in Your holy name, Amen.

—BILLY GRAHAM

JESUS CHRIST

(ca. 4 BC–30 AD)

Jesus Christ is undoubtedly the most controversial figure in human history. Jesus was born in Bethlehem, in Palestine's West Bank, in approximately 4 BC. The Bible teaches that He was conceived by the Holy Spirit and born to the Virgin Mary (Matthew 1:20, 25; Luke 1:26–35). Joseph, Mary's betrothed husband, would serve as Jesus' earthly father.

Jesus' life was tumultuous from the very beginning. Mary and Joseph were forced to flee as refugees to Egypt when Herod the Great, in an effort to kill Jesus, ordered that all infants under age two be murdered. The family stayed in Egypt until Herod's death and then settled in Nazareth.

Little is known about Jesus' adolescent years. Luke 3:23 recounts that Jesus' ministry started when He was around thirty. He was baptized by John the Baptist, who announced that Jesus was the Lamb of God, who takes away the sins of the world (John 1:29). After Jesus' baptism, He spent forty days fasting in the wilderness and was tempted by the enemy. On three separate

occasions, the enemy tempted Jesus, and the Gospels testify that Jesus overcame the devil by speaking the Word of God (Matthew 4:1–11).

The four Gospels chronicle Jesus' life and ministry, which included miraculous healings, preaching of the gospel, and making disciples out of His followers. The Scriptures teach that Jesus was convicted of blasphemy for claiming to be God, He was crucified on a Roman cross, and on the third day, He rose from the dead. Christians believe Jesus Christ to be the Son of God, the Messiah, and the Savior of the world. The most well-known scripture testifies of this: "For God so loved the world that he gave his one and only Son, that whoever believes in him shall not perish but have eternal life" (John 3:16 NIV).

Our Father in heaven,

Hallowed be Your name.

Your kingdom come.

Your will be done

On earth as it is in heaven.

Give us this day our daily bread.

And forgive us our debts,

As we forgive our debtors.

And do not lead us into temptation,

But deliver us from the evil one.

For Yours is the kingdom and the power and the

glory forever.

Amen.

—Jesus Christ, found in Matthew 6:9–13

HELEN KELLER

(1880–1968)

On June 27, 1880, Helen Keller was born a healthy infant in Tuscumbia, Alabama. When she was nineteen months old, she became blind and deaf as a result of an undiagnosed illness.

In 1887, Helen's life changed when Anne Sullivan moved to Tuscumbia to be her teacher. Helen had become an unruly child, and Anne believed she needed to be guided by obedience and love. Anne taught Helen sign language by forming the letters of the alphabet in Helen's hand, and Helen later learned to speak.

Helen's skills were notable from even a young age, and despite the odds, in 1904, she became the first deaf-blind person to earn a bachelor of arts degree when she graduated cum laude from Radcliffe College. It was in while college that Helen began her writing career. Her autobiography, *The Story of My Life*, is still in print and has been translated into fifty languages.

Above all things, Helen considered herself a writer, and it was through

her writing and public speaking that she advocated for the rights of the underdog, including the disabled.

In 1924, she joined the American Foundation for the Blind (AFB) and worked for the organization for more than forty years. AFB provided her a global platform that she used to advocate for those with vision loss. She visited thirty-five countries on five continents in her relentless pursuits on behalf of the disabled and broke down barriers as she pushed for changes in laws that made it possible for those with disabilities to move into mainstream education. "I will not just live my life," she vowed. "I will not just spend my life. I will invest my life."

*For three things I thank God every day
of my life: that He has vouchsafed my
knowledge of His works; deep thanks that
He has set in my darkness the lamp of faith;
deep, deepest thanks that I have another
life to look forward to—a life joyous with
light and flowers and heavenly song.*

—Helen Keller

THOMAS À KEMPIS

(1380–1471)

Thomas à Kempis was born in the fourteenth century, an age when war was ever present and the bubonic plague had drastically reduced the population. He joined a Dutch Augustinian monastery affiliated with the Brethren of the Common Life, a Catholic religious community. As the prior's assistant, Thomas was responsible for providing spiritual instruction to the novices in the community. It was during this assignment, between 1420 and 1427, that Thomas wrote four books, which collectively became *The Imitation of Christ*, the most popular devotional book ever written.

The praises of this classic are many. John Wesley, the father of the Methodist Church, described it as the finest summary of the Christian life he had ever read. Jesuits founder Ignatius of Loyola read from it daily and bought additional copies to be given as gifts. And Sir Thomas More, councillor to England's Henry VIII, identified the book as one that everyone should own.

By the end of the fifteenth century, *The Imitation of Christ* had been published in English, Latin, German, French, Italian, and Spanish, and by 1779, there were already eighteen hundred editions. Today the classic devotional has been translated into more than fifty languages.

In this most famous work, Thomas taught that the most important virtue, the one from which all others develop, is humility. What a fitting lesson—then and now.

Grant me, sweet Jesus, to rest in You above every
creature; above all health and beauty, above all glory
and honor, above all power and dignity, above all
knowledge and skillfulness, above all riches and
arts, above all joy and exultation, above all fame
and praise, above all sweetness and consolation,
above all hope and promise, above all gifts that You
can give, above all joy the mind is able to receive;
above everything that You, O my God, are not.

—Thomas à Kempis

MARTIN LUTHER KING JR.

(1929–1968)

M artin Luther King Jr. is widely regarded as American's leading advocate for nonviolence and one of the greatest leaders in world history. Dr. King led the American civil rights movement from December 1955 until his untimely death on April 4, 1968. During those thirteen years, more advances were made toward racial equality in America than in the previous 350 years combined.

Born on January 15, 1929, at the family home in Atlanta to the Reverend Martin Luther King Sr. and Alberta Williams King, the young boy grew up to follow his father into the ministry. In 1951, he moved to Boston to attend school. While there, he began dating Coretta Scott, a student at the New England Conservatory of Music. They married in 1953. In 1955, he graduated with a doctorate in systematic theology from Boston University School of Theology.

During the late 1950s, Dr. King launched a campaign to achieve legal

equality for African Americans in the United States. His strategy involved utilizing acts of nonviolent resistance, the power of communication, and grassroots efforts, which together achieved seemingly impossible goals. Dr. King also served as the spokesperson for the Montgomery Bus Boycott, which ultimately led to the end of racial segregation on public transportation. In 1963, he led the March on Washington, which drew 250,000 people to the national mall and influenced Congress to pass the Civil Rights Act, making it illegal to discriminate against minorities.

Dr. King's "I Have a Dream Speech" and his "Letters from a Birmingham Jail" are among the most revered messages in American history. He is the only non-president to have a national holiday to memorialize him, and at age thirty-five he became the youngest ever recipient of the Nobel Peace Prize.

O God, . . . we thank Thee for Thy Church, founded

upon Thy Word, that challenges us to do more than

sing and pray, but go out and work as though the

very answer to our prayers depended on us and not

upon Thee. . . . Help us to realize that man was

created to shine like the stars and live on through

all eternity. Keep us, we pray, in perfect peace, help

us to walk together, pray together, sing together,

and live together until that day when all God's

children, Black, White, Red, and Yellow, will rejoice

in one common band of humanity in the kingdom

of our Lord and of our God, we pray. Amen.

—MARTIN LUTHER KING JR.

JOHN KNOX

(ca. 1513–1572)

John Knox, the founder of the Presbyterian denomination and a key figure in the formation of modern Scotland, was born around 1513 in the small community of Haddington, near Edinburgh, during a time of great transition in his country. The Scots had become frustrated with the Catholic Church, which owned more than 50 percent of the real estate and outearned the crown by a wide margin. Soon the religious landscape of the country would change forever.

Knox began theological studies around 1529 at the University of St. Andrews, becoming an ordained minister in 1536. In the 1540s, heavily influenced by the reformers, Knox joined their ranks.

In 1547, Knox and other Protestants were arrested and sent to the galleys as slaves. Knox remained enslaved for nineteen months. After his release, Knox spent five years in England, gaining a reputation as an

outspoken preacher. Meanwhile, in Scotland, Protestantism was growing, and its adherents vowed to make it the religion of the land.

By 1560, the future of Protestantism was assured in Scotland, and Parliament ordered Knox and five of his peers to write a Protestant confession of faith, a book of discipline, and a directory for public worship. These guiding documents led Scotland in a new, distinctly Presbyterian and Calvinist direction.

Today there are approximately 750,000 Presbyterians in Scotland, three million in the United States, and millions more across the globe.

Because we have need continually to crave many things at Your hands, we humbly beg You, O heavenly Father, to grant us Your Holy Spirit to direct our petitions, that they may proceed from such a fervent mind as may be agreeable to Your holy will. Amen.

—John Knox

JARENA LEE

(1783–1864)

———————————

Jarena Lee was the first African American woman to publicly preach the gospel, and she did so in an era when slavery was still legal and neither African Americans nor women had the right to vote.

Lee was born on February 11, 1783, in Cape May, New Jersey. Although she was born free, she grew up separated from her parents by sixty miles because of her work as a maid.

A couple of years after becoming a Christian, Lee shared her desire to preach with Richard Allen, founder of the African Methodist Episcopal Church. At the time, Allen didn't feel comfortable allowing a woman to preach from his pulpit. Eight years later, he would change his mind.

In 1817, the Reverend Richard Williams was scheduled to preach on a Sunday morning, but at the last minute, he was unable to deliver the sermon. Lee rose from her seat and spoke to the congregation. She later wrote, "During the exhortation, God made manifest His power in a manner

sufficient to show the world that I was called to labor according to my ability, and the grace given unto me, in the vineyard of the good husbandman."

Bishop Allen was seated in the congregation that day and after hearing Lee was convinced that God had called her to preach. This was the beginning of Lee's preaching ministry.

Lee's audience proved diverse. She preached to racially mixed crowds of Methodists, Baptists, Presbyterians, and Wesleyan groups in lower Canada, the mid-Atlantic states, New England, and the cities of Detroit and Cincinnati. Lee preached for more than twenty years before illness began to impact her schedule. She died in 1949, shortly after publishing the third revision of her autobiography.

Today Lee is not only considered a trailblazer for African Americans but a pioneer for women in ministry.

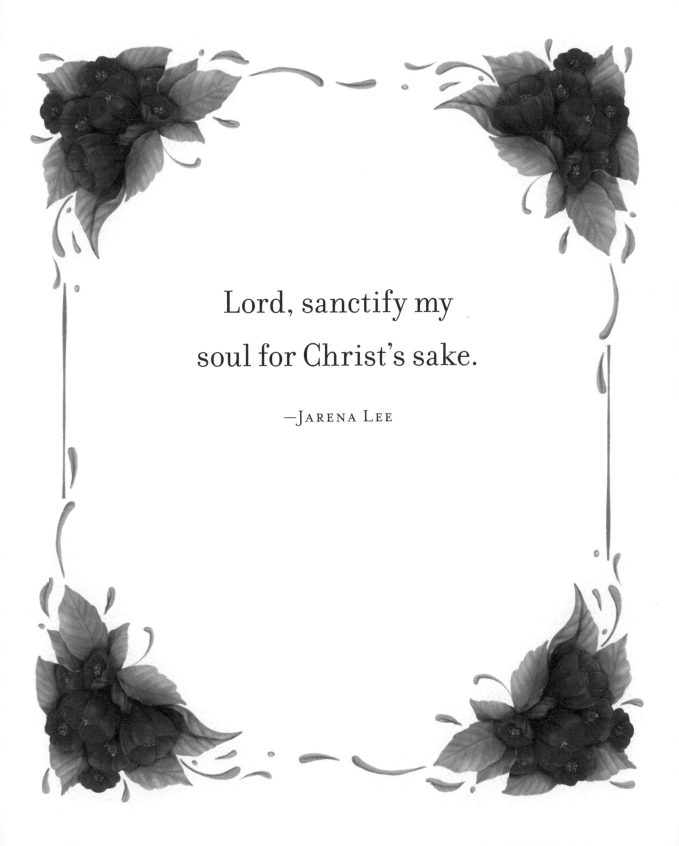

Lord, sanctify my
soul for Christ's sake.

—Jarena Lee

C. S. LEWIS

(1898–1963)

C. S. Lewis is known as one of the greatest Christian writers of the twentieth century, but as a young man, he was an avowed atheist.

Lewis was born on November 29, 1898, in Belfast, Ireland, to a family of intellectuals known for their voracious reading habits. Growing up, Lewis was a loner, spending hours reading books and writing and illustrating his own stories. Shortly after his tenth birthday, his mother died of cancer. Her death had a significant impact on young "Jack," as he was called, and his father never recovered, instead withdrawing from Lewis and his brother, Warren. Their home life was never the same. Lewis concluded that God was either cruel, passively removed, or nonexistent.

In 1917, Lewis began his studies at Oxford and just two years later published his first book under the pseudonym Clive Hamilton. Though he rejected the claims of Christianity, he found himself drawn to Christian writers George MacDonald and G. K. Chesterton.

After graduating, Lewis joined the English faculty at Magdalen College. There he met Christians Hugo Dyson and J. R. R. Tolkien. The three became close friends.

Between the logic of his favored authors and conversations with his new friends, Lewis's thoughts were stirred and his atheism challenged. In 1929, Lewis surrendered, admitting, "God was God," and he knelt and prayed for the first time in years. Eventually he also embraced the Christian faith.

Although Lewis went on to enjoy great success in his writing career, even close friends often criticized him for his Christian lifestyle. On more than one occasion he was passed over for professorship at Oxford. Finally, in 1955, Magdalen College at Cambridge recognized him for his literary contributions and honored Lewis with a chair.

Lewis became one of the world's most beloved Christian apologists and authored more than thirty books, including the Christian classics *Mere Christianity*, *The Screwtape Letters*, and his famed Chronicles of Narnia fiction series.

Take not, O Lord, our literal sense,

but in Thy great,

Unbroken speech our halting

metaphor translate.

—C. S. Lewis

ABRAHAM LINCOLN

(1809–1865)

In 1861, Abraham Lincoln became the sixteenth president of the United States, yet Lincoln came to office with no presidential pedigree. He was born in Hardin County, Kentucky, from, in his words, "undistinguished families." His mother died when he was ten, and he spent his early years working on a farm. Even then, Lincoln went to great lengths to gain knowledge, eventually becoming a lawyer. His law partner said of him, "His ambition was a little engine that knew no rest."

In time, he married Mary Todd, and though they had four sons, only one survived to adulthood.

Lincoln ran for senator against Democrat Stephen A. Douglas in the 1858 election. Though he lost, the reputation he earned during his debates with Douglas ultimately won him the Republican nomination for the 1860 presidential election, an election that Lincoln won.

During Lincoln's time as president, the Republican Party gained

momentum and became a strong national establishment. His crowning achievement was the Emancipation Proclamation, issued on January 1, 1863, which ordered freedom for all slaves.

Lincoln's untimely death came on Good Friday, April 14, 1865, when actor John Wilkes Booth shot him. But Lincoln's name lives on, and America was bettered by his presidency.

Fondly do we hope, fervently do we pray, that this mighty scourge of war may speedily pass away. Yet, if God wills that it continue . . . until every drop of blood drawn with the lash shall be paid by another drawn with the sword . . . so still it must be said "the judgments of the Lord are true and righteous altogether." With malice toward none, with charity for all, with firmness in the right as God gives us to see the right, let us strive on to finish the work we are in, to bind up the nation's wounds, to care for him who shall have borne the battle and for his widow and his orphan, to do all which may achieve and cherish a just and lasting peace among ourselves and with all nations.

—ABRAHAM LINCOLN, SECOND INAUGURAL
ADDRESS, MARCH 4, 1865

MARTIN LUTHER

(1483–1546)

M artin Luther is known as the father of the Protestant Reformation. Few people in Christian history have been as influential and controversial.

Luther was a German monk in the sixteenth century. In 1517, he began to question some of the basic tenets of Roman Catholicism. His departure from Catholicism began when he publicly objected to the church's sale of indulgences, documents that would allegedly release the purchasers or their deceased loved ones from the penalty of their sins. In a call for reform, Luther drafted his famous Ninety-Five Theses and requested a public debate. In the meantime, his theses were widely circulated throughout Germany, and Luther gained support. Soon the Catholic Church, incensed by Luther's challenge to Church authority, was calling for his excommunication. Ultimately, Luther and his followers split from the Roman Catholic Church, and the Protestant tradition was born.

Luther was reputedly irritable and argumentative, and in his later years

he suffered from poor health, but his contributions to theology and music continued to accumulate. He translated the Bible into German, published a large body of work, and even wrote a number of hymns, including the classic "A Mighty Fortress Is Our God." The Protestant Reformers who followed Luther were heavily influenced by his work, as are theologians today.

Luther was known as a man of prayer and on one of his busiest days resolved to spend his first three hours in prayer. "To be a Christian without prayer," he said, "is no more possible than to be alive without breathing."

Oh Lord, help me. Strengthen my faith and trust in You. In You I have sealed all the treasures I have. I am poor; You are rich and came to be merciful to the poor. I am a sinner; You are upright. With me there is an abundance of sin; in You is the fullness of righteousness. Therefore, I will remain with You from whom I can receive, but to whom I may not give. Amen.

—MARTIN LUTHER

AIMEE SEMPLE McPHERSON

(1890–1944)

Historians consider Aimee Semple McPherson among the most significant revivalists of the early twentieth century.

In October 1890, Aimee was born in Ontario, Canada, to James and Minnie Kennedy. During her teen years, she was introduced to Pentecostalism through the preaching of Robert Semple, whom she would eventually marry. After Semple died, just two years into their marriage, Aimee married businessman Harold McPherson.

For a time, the McPhersons traveled in a "gospel" car covered with Bible verses, and they handed out religious tracts. Aimee preached and began drawing crowds. Soon she caught the eye of the press. But in the meantime, her marriage was failing.

Aimee and Harold divorced quietly, but Aimee's ministry flourished as she faithfully preached "the four-square Gospel" (Jesus as the only Savior, the Great Physician, the Baptizer with the Holy Spirit, and the coming

Bridegroom). Her audiences were captivated by her speaking skills, and the press marveled. Her crowds continued to grow, and in 1919, she held a series of meetings in Los Angeles that launched her to national fame.

In May 1926, McPherson's momentum was halted when she disappeared. It was announced that she had gone swimming and never returned, leaving people to assume she'd drowned. A memorial was held in her honor. Three days after the memorial, she reappeared at the Mexico-Arizona border and claimed she had been kidnapped but escaped. Her account could not be verified, and what happened during this time period is still a mystery.

The following January McPherson set out on another evangelistic tour and continued to minister until her death from accidental overdose compounded by kidney failure on her fifty-fourth birthday. Her ongoing legacy is the denomination she founded, the International Church of the Foursquare Gospel, which has two million members and close to thirty thousand churches globally.

O Hope! dazzling, radiant Hope!—What a change Thou bringest to the hopeless, brightening the darkened paths, and cheering the lonely way.

—Aimee Semple McPherson

DWIGHT MOODY

(1837–1899)

Dwight Moody was one of the greatest evangelists of the nineteenth century, which seemed unlikely during his early life on the family's Massachusetts farm. Moody's father died when he was just four, leaving his mother, Betsey, to raise nine children. Growing up, Moody wasn't encouraged to explore his faith, and he only finished the equivalent of a fifth-grade education. At age seventeen, Moody started work as a shoe salesman at his uncle's Boston store. Meanwhile, he attended Sunday school classes at the YMCA, and at eighteen, he became a Christian.

Shortly after his conversion, he moved to Chicago. As his faith continued to grow, Moody founded a Sunday school at North Market Hall in a poverty-stricken area of the city. It flourished, and the church that developed was the precursor to the now famous Moody Memorial Church. Moody married one of the Sunday school teachers, Emma C. Revell, and they had three children.

Moody became president of the YMCA and deepened his ministry ties in the city. Unfortunately, the Great Chicago Fire destroyed Moody's church, his home, and the YMCA in 1871. Moody then felt called to devote all of his time to evangelism.

An opportunity for Moody to preach abroad arose following the untimely deaths of two Anglican evangelists. When Moody returned to America two years later, he was an internationally known evangelist. Moody traveled back and forth between Europe and America and preached to more than a hundred million people.

In 1866, Moody founded the Moody Bible Institute and would later open Moody Press. He remained tireless in his efforts to share the gospel and preached up to six sermons a day until a month before his death.

Our heavenly Father, we pray that Thy blessing may rest upon each one of us gathered here now and as we go hence. We pray that the Spirit of the Lord God may come down upon each one of us, and that we may each one of us turn away from every sin. O God, forgive us for our selfishness, forgive us for the stint of self-seeking. O God, keep us from this way, so that we may not be seeking sacred things for ourselves, but that we may bow ourselves in the dust before Thee today. Help us to draw near to Thee. We pray Thee that Thou wilt give us power from on high, for Thou dost remember our frame; Thou knowest that we are dust, and Thou knowest how prone we are to wander. O God, give us the victory over ourselves; give us grace from above every day and hour to glorify Thee. We pray now for Thy blessing to rest upon us as we go hence. Amen.

—DWIGHT MOODY

LOTTIE MOON

(1840–1912)

Lottie Moon, a name that is synonymous with the Southern Baptists' international missions offering, was a longtime missionary to China who advocated for women's involvement in sharing the gospel around the world.

She was born Charlotte Diggs Moon in December 1840 in Virginia. As an adolescent, she rebelled against Christianity, but in 1858, she committed her life to following Christ. Moon attended school at Virginia's Albemarle Female Institute. In 1861, she became one of the first women in the South to earn a master's degree.

At age thirty-two, Moon was appointed as a missionary to Tengchow, China. She turned down a marriage proposal and left her job and family to obey God's lead. Moon would serve as a missionary for thirty-nine years, predominantly in the province of Shantung. She also taught in a girls' school and frequently made trips into China's interior to share the gospel with women and girls.

Moon wrote letters home describing the spiritual hunger she was witnessing in China and the problem of having so few missionaries to communicate the gospel to the 472 million people there at the time. She shared the need for more workers and urged the Southern Baptists to offer their support through prayer and giving. In a letter to the Foreign Mission Board, she wrote, "Please say to the new missionaries they are coming to a life of hardship, responsibility, and constant self-denial."

Moon died at the age of seventy-two after decades of faithful service. But her legacy continues, and the Lottie Moon Christmas offering, begun in 1918, continues today.

I pray that no missionary will ever be as lonely as I have been.

—Lottie Moon

GEORGE MÜLLER

(1805–1898)

No one thought teenage George Müller had a future. By age sixteen, Müller, a native German, had already spent time in jail for theft. But after several tumultuous years, a friend invited him to a Saturday-night Bible study, and Müller later described that night as the turning point in his life. At twenty-one, Müller submitted to the lordship of Christ and dedicated his life to full-time ministry.

In 1830, Müller married Mary Groves, and the newlyweds moved to Bristol, England, in 1832 to begin work at Bethesda Chapel, where Müller preached until his death. While in Bristol, Müller felt moved to care for the poor and was drawn to the orphans living on the city streets. He and his wife began plans to take in thirty children in their rented home, and eventually, in an effort to help more children, the couple opened five orphanages.

Most notably, Müller committed to never soliciting donations on behalf of the orphanages, but instead chose only to take his needs to God in prayer.

Stories of last-minute provisions and unlikely contributions are legendary in Müller's ministry. By the time of his death, Müller's orphanages had housed more than 10,000 children, and he had built 117 schools that had educated more than 120,000 children.

Of his prayer life, Müller said, "I live in the spirit of prayer. I pray as I walk about, when I lie down and when I rise up. And the answers are always coming. Thousands and tens of thousands of times have my prayers been answered. When once I am persuaded that a thing is right and for the glory of God, I go on praying for it until the answer comes."

May the Lord grant, that the eyes of many of His children may be opened, so that they may seek, in all spiritual things, to be separated from unbelievers, and to do God's work according to God's mind!

—George Müller

JOHN NEWTON

(1725–1807)

When the former slave trader and English clergyman John Newton wrote "Amazing Grace," he penned the most famous hymn in history.

Newton was raised by his Christian mother, who taught him the Bible when he was young. But Newton's mother died of tuberculosis when he was only seven, and after that, his father, a sea captain, raised him. When Newton turned eleven, he embarked on his first of six sea voyages with him.

In his adolescent years, Newton had problems with authority and got fired from his first job. It was a pattern that would repeat itself time and again. He went to work with a slave trader, and for years he continued to be arrogant and disrespectful toward authority.

In 1747, Newton was aboard a ship traveling to Liverpool when it sailed into a storm. Fearing for his life, Newton converted to Christianity in the midst of the storm, though he later said that at that point he couldn't consider himself a genuine believer.

Newton served as a mate and later as a captain on numerous slave ships. In 1755, Newton left the ships for a desk job, and as he grew in his faith, he became increasingly sickened by the slave trade and his onetime role in the trade. He quit his job and became an ordained minister.

Newton began writing hymns for a weekly Bible study in 1769, and among those he wrote was "Amazing Grace." Newton was remorseful over his participation in the slave trade and considered the lyrics of this song to be autobiographical. It is still sung in churches the world over.

Amazing grace, how sweet the sound,

That saved a wretch like me.

I once was lost, but now am found,

Was blind but now I see.

—JOHN NEWTON, "AMAZING GRACE"

REINHOLD NIEBUHR

(1892–1971)

R einhold Niebuhr was one of the most influential American theologians of the twentieth century. He was born in Missouri in 1892 to a German-born minister of the German Evangelical Synod of North America. Niebuhr, a committed liberal, received his own theological training at Synod's Eden Theological Seminary and at Yale Divinity School.

In the 1920s, Niebuhr pastored a church in Detroit, Michigan, home to an intense labor-capital conflict. Niebuhr sympathized with the unions, and he became a member of the Norman Thomas Socialist Party. His teachings and writings got the attention of New York's Union Theological Seminary, and in 1928, they invited Niebuhr to be a member of their faculty. He accepted the position and taught there until his death in 1971.

Though a pastor at heart, Niebuhr was also keenly interested in social and political affairs. He was an advocate for what became known as the "social gospel," which served as a blueprint for progressive social reform.

Niebuhr made an enormous impact on political thought both inside and outside the church. He left behind an impressive body of work, including his two-volume *Nature and Destiny of Man*. Millions of people who may not know his name are familiar with Niebuhr's theology through his familiar "serenity prayer," which continues to be one of the most well-known prayers of all time.

God, give us grace to accept
with serenity the things that
cannot be changed, courage
to change the things that
should be changed, and
the wisdom to distinguish
the one from the other.

—Reinhold Niebuhr

HENRI NOUWEN

(1932–1996)

⁂

Henri Nouwen felt called to the priesthood at a young age. Born on January 24, 1932, in Nijkerk, Holland, he was ordained as a Catholic priest and was a psychology major at the Catholic University of Nijmegen. He moved to the United States in 1964 to further his education. After completing his studies at the Menninger Clinic in Topeka, Kansas, he taught at the University of Notre Dame and later at the divinity schools of Harvard and Yale, becoming an esteemed professor in his field.

In 1985, at the height of Nouwen's academic career, he felt called to join L'Arche in Trosly, France. It was a sacrifice few would make. L'Arche was the first of more than a hundred communities for people with intellectual disabilities. The following year, Nouwen made his home at L'Arche Daybreak near Toronto, Ontario.

Nouwen is the author of thirty-nine books on the spiritual life. He routinely communicated in English, French, German, Dutch, and Spanish

with countless friends, and he reached thousands through his lectures, retreats, and Eucharist celebrations.

Since Nouwen's sudden death in 1996, increasing numbers of readers, pastors, writers, teachers, and seekers have been influenced by his literary legacy. His books have been published in more than twenty-eight languages and sold more than eight million copies.

Dear God,

I am so afraid to open my clenched fists!

Who will I be when I have nothing left to hold on to?

Who will I be when I stand before You with empty

 hands?

Please help me to gradually open my hands and to

 discover that I am not what I own,

but what You want to give me.

And what You want to give me is love—

unconditional, everlasting love.

Amen.

—Henri Nouwen

ROSA PARKS

(1913–2005)

In 1955, Rosa Parks, an African American seamstress, refused to give up her seat to a white man on a city bus in Montgomery, Alabama. Her act of bravery and defiance of the city's "Jim Crow" laws helped launch the civil rights movement in America and made her a nationally recognized symbol of resilience and dignity in the effort to end racial segregation.

Rosa Louise McCauley was born on February 4, 1913, in Tuskegee, Alabama, to James and Leona McCauley. When Rosa was eleven, the family moved to Montgomery, Alabama, and Rosa attended school there. She was forced to leave school in the eleventh grade to care for her dying grandmother and then to tend to her chronically ill mother.

At nineteen, Rosa married barber Raymond Parks, who was a longtime member of the National Association for the Advancement of Colored People (NAACP). With Raymond's encouragement, Rosa earned her high school

diploma the following year. A few years later, she also joined the NAACP and became the chapter secretary.

On December 1, 1955, Rosa, at forty-two, made history when she refused to forfeit her seat to a white man while commuting home after her shift at the Montgomery Fair department store. She was arrested and taken into custody. Though she was released later the same evening, her arrest caused outrage in the black community and sparked the Montgomery bus boycott. Parks lost her job and was then subjected to continual harassment. Finally, on November 13, 1956, the Supreme Court ruled that bus segregation was unconstitutional. Parks became known as a leader and "the mother of the civil rights movement."

I am bound for the freedom land,

I am bound for the freedom land

O who will come and go with me?

I am bound for the freedom land.

On Jordan's stormy banks I stand,

And cast a wishful eye;

To Canaan's fair and freedom land,

Where my possessions lie.

—Rosa Parks, revised lyrics to the hymn

"I Am Bound for the Promised Land"

SAINT PATRICK

(ca. 385–461)

———

Saint Patrick is often associated with the annual parades held in his honor. In reality, he was a humble missionary who evangelized Ireland and set off a chain of events that would affect all of Europe.

At sixteen, Patrick was captured from his home in Scotland and spent six years in slavery after being sold to a brutal warrior chief. As a slave, he often endured long periods of thirst and hunger. But it was in captivity that his faith grew and he sought the Christian God of his fathers for relief.

In his early twenties, Patrick escaped from his captor and traveled to Ireland as a missionary. Whether or not he was the first missionary to Ireland is a matter of debate, but it is certain that when Patrick arrived in Ireland, paganism dominated the land. He faced intense opposition from the druids, who practiced magic and who "wished to kill the holy Patrick."

Patrick was also an outspoken critic of slavery, and historians agree it was he who wrote a letter excommunicating the British tyrant Coroticus,

who had taken some of Patrick's converts into slavery. Despite his successes as a missionary, he continued to struggle with self-doubt and believed he was not worthy to be a bishop.

Irish annals report that Patrick died in 493, when he would have been in his seventies. His greatest achievement was being one of the first missionaries to communicate the gospel outside the boundaries of Roman civilization.

Christ with me, Christ before me, Christ

behind me;

Christ within me, Christ beneath me, Christ

above me;

Christ to the right of me, Christ to the left of me;

Christ in my lying, Christ in my sitting, Christ in

my rising;

Christ in the heart of all who think of me,

Christ on the tongue of all who speak to me,

Christ in the eye of all who see me,

Christ in the ear of all who hear me.

—SAINT PATRICK

POLYCARP

(69–156)

———————————

Polycarp is the first recorded martyr to die for his faith in post–New Testament history. He lived during a pivotal time for the early church, when the era of the original apostles came to a close and the church was transitioning to the second generation of believers. According to tradition, he was discipled by the apostle John, and others among the original apostles appointed him as bishop of Smyrna. A letter he wrote to the church at Philippi, his only piece of existing writing, reveals that although he had little formal education, he was assertive.

Polycarp took on a formative role as a leader as he attempted to settle disagreements about when to celebrate Easter and confronted the gnostic Marcion, who was widely known as one of the church's most problematic heretics.

Polycarp had been a Christian since his childhood but didn't come under the scrutiny of the Romans until he was nearing ninety. Although loved ones urged him to flee, when Roman authorities discovered his location, Polycarp let the soldiers inside and replied, "God's will be done." He was sentenced to be burned at the stake.

As the soldiers prepared to nail him to the stake, Polycarp said, "Leave me as I am. For He who grants me to endure the fire will enable me also to remain on the pyre unmoved, without the security from your nails." Polycarp prayed aloud as the fire was lit and consumed his flesh. Tradition holds that Polycarp's martyrdom was remembered by "everyone," even the heathen.

O Lord God Almighty, Father of Your beloved and blessed servant Jesus Christ, through whom we have received knowledge of You, the God of angels and powers and of all creation, and of the whole race of the righteous who live in Your presence: I bless You because You have considered me worthy of this day and hour, that I might receive a place among the martyrs and share in the cup of Christ, for resurrection to eternal life, for soul and body in the incorruptibility of the Holy Spirit. Among them may I be accepted before You today, as a rich and acceptable sacrifice, just as You, the faithful and true God, have prepared and foreshown and brought about. For this reason and for all things I praise You, I bless You, I glorify You, through the eternal heavenly high priest Jesus Christ, Your beloved child, through whom be glory to You, with Him and the Holy Spirit, now and for the ages to come. Amen.

—POLYCARP, A PRAYER BEFORE BEING
BURNED AT THE STAKE

CHARLES SPURGEON

(1834–1892)

—————✦—————

Charles Haddon Spurgeon is known as the "Prince of Preachers" with good reason. The Baptist pastor published more than thirty-five hundred sermons and preached to an estimated ten million people during his lifetime, which is a staggering number, especially in a pre-internet era.

Spurgeon was raised in a Christian home but attributed his conversion to a sermon he heard when he was fifteen while stranded at a chapel during a snowstorm. He preached his first sermon later the same year.

Although Spurgeon didn't have a formal college education, he was an avid reader and eventually accumulated more than twelve thousand books in his personal library.

Spurgeon was known for his superior work ethic, and there were seasons during his ministry when he preached as many as thirteen times a week. His preaching drew huge crowds, and many came to Christ. Spurgeon also authored a large body of work, publishing more than eighteen million

words and selling more than fifty-six million copies of his sermons, in nearly forty languages.

In addition to his preaching ministry and his writing, Spurgeon was the founder of the famous Stockwell Orphanage, and he supported numerous charitable outreaches, including his Pastor's College, which educated nine hundred students in Spurgeon's era and still exists today.

In June 1891, Spurgeon preached his last sermon. He died six months later. During his three-day wake in January 1892, nearly 60,000 people came to pay their respects, and 100,000 lined the streets as the hearse carried his body to the cemetery.

Lord, slay sloth within us, and never let us find a pillow in the doctrines of grace for ease while yet a single sin remains. . . . O keep us, we beseech Thee, Lord, for without Thy keeping we cannot keep ourselves.

—CHARLES SPURGEON

HARRIET BEECHER STOWE

(1811–1896)

———✦———

Harriet Beecher Stowe is the author of the classic *Uncle Tom's Cabin*. In 1863, when President Abraham Lincoln met Harriet, he reportedly said, "So you're the little woman who wrote the book that made this great war!" Although the book can't be blamed for starting the Civil War, Stowe's writing communicated the value of the human soul and paved the way for inevitable emancipation.

Stowe was born the seventh of twelve children. Her father, Lyman Beecher, was a Congregationalist minister and noted reformer and revivalist. Her mother died when Stowe was young, and her father moved the family to Cincinnati.

When Stowe was twenty-five, she married Calvin Ellis Stowe, a professor of biblical literature, and they had seven children together. She read to her children two hours each night.

Stowe found time to write between household chores so she could

bolster the limited family income. She wrote continually and experienced some successes early on. Her husband encouraged her writing, and when she was forty, she finished *Uncle Tom's Cabin*. Through this historic novel and its main character, the slave Tom, Stowe was able to communicate the ludicrousness of slavery. The book enjoyed unprecedented success and was translated into at least twenty-three languages. By the time of the Civil War, it had already sold a million copies.

Stowe continued to write and averaged a book a year until her death in July 1896, but *Uncle Tom's Cabin* is her legacy. One of her most vocal critics admitted that it was "perhaps the most influential novel ever published, a verbal earthquake, an ink-and-paper tidal wave."

When winds are raging o'er the upper ocean,

And billows wild contend with angry roar,

'Tis said, far down, beneath the wild commotion,

That peaceful stillness reigneth evermore. . . .

O rest of rests! O peace serene, eternal!

Thou ever livest and Thou changest never;

And in the secret of Thy presence dwelleth

Fulness of joy, forever and forever.

—Harriet Beecher Stowe

MOTHER TERESA OF CALCUTTA

(1910–1997)

⁂

The woman known to the world as "Mother Teresa" was born Agnes Gonxha Bojaxhiu on August 26, 1910, in Skopje, Macedonia. Her father died when she was eight, leaving her mother to support the family with her embroidery and cloth business.

As a child, she was deeply involved in parish activities before leaving home in 1928 for the Loreto Convent in Dublin, Ireland, where she was enrolled as a postulant and given the name of Teresa.

She arrived in Calcutta, India (Kolkata today), in January 1929, at the behest of the Loreto order. On May 24, 1937, she made her final profession as a Loreto nun and from that point on was called Mother Teresa. Throughout the 1930s and 1940s, she taught at St. Mary's Bengali Medium School.

It was on a train ride from Calcutta to Darjeeling that Mother Teresa received what she described as "a call within the call" to serve the poor. To fulfill this call, she founded an institute, the Missionaries of Charity, the

mission of which was "to quench the infinite thirst of Jesus on the cross for love and souls by laboring at the salvation and sanctification of the poorest of the poor."

In 1970, Mother Teresa was awarded the Nobel Peace Prize. By 1997, she had established almost six hundred foundations in 123 countries.

In the summer of 1997, after a busy time of travel, Mother Teresa returned to Calcutta in poor health. On September 5, she died at the Motherhouse, sixty-nine years after first arriving in India. Hundreds of thousands of people from across India and abroad came to pay their respects alongside presidents, royalty, and prime ministers. Mother Teresa had dedicated her life to serving the poor and disenfranchised, and in death, she was remembered by all.

Oh Jesus, You who suffer, grant that today and every day
I may be able to see You in the person of Your sick ones
and that, by offering them my care, I may serve You.
Grant that, even if You are hidden under the
unattractive disguise of anger, of crime, or of
madness, I may recognize You and say, "Jesus,
You who suffer, how sweet it is to serve You."
Give me, Lord, this vision of faith, and my work will
never be monotonous. I will find joy in harboring the
small whims and desires of all the poor who suffer. . . .
Lord, increase my faith. Bless my efforts
and my work, now and forever.

—MOTHER TERESA OF CALCUTTA

SOJOURNER TRUTH

(ca. 1797–1883)

———————————

Sojourner Truth was born a slave named Isabella Baumfree in southeastern New York. During her early years, she was subjected to several slave owners, many of whom were cruel. When Truth turned thirteen, she was bought by John Dumont and worked for him for seventeen years before escaping to the home of Isaac and Maria Van Wagener. Truth later said God had revealed them to her in a vision. The Quaker couple purchased Truth from Dumont and then freed her.

A fresh start warranted a new name, and she prayed God would provide one. She said that God showed her in a vision that her new name was Sojourner, because of the traveling she would do as a speaker, and that she was to declare Truth to the people. Truth became an abolitionist and traveled throughout the Northeast, attending local prayer meetings and organizing meetings of her own. She spoke against the evils of slavery and on behalf of women's rights.

In 1850, with the help of Olive Gilbert, she published her autobiography. The book brought her both fame and harassment. Following a physical attack from a violent mob, she walked with a cane for the rest of her life.

By the time the Civil War ended, Truth had made numerous speeches on behalf of minorities and women, met with Abraham Lincoln, called on the government to make western lands available to freed African Americans, and suffered a dislocated arm at the hands of a racist streetcar conductor. She settled in Battle Creek, Michigan, and made it her home until her death.

Oh, God, You know how much I am distressed, for I have told You again and again. Now, God, help me get my son. If You were in trouble, as I am, and I could help You, as You can me, think I wouldn't do it? Yes, God, You know I would do it. Oh, God, You know I have no money, but You can make the people do for me, and You must make the people do for me. I will never give You peace till You do, God. Oh God, make the people hear me—don't let them turn me off, without hearing and helping me.

—Sojourner Truth

HARRIET TUBMAN

(ca. 1820–1913)

Harriet Tubman was raised a slave in eastern Maryland, a slave state. She escaped in 1849, but when she arrived in the North, she was not satisfied with her own freedom but longed to help those still trapped in slavery. Harriet returned to the South on nineteen trips and helped at least three hundred fellow slaves escape. Her mission to lead so many to freedom via the Underground Railroad earned her the nickname "Moses."

Tubman made her heroic rescue trips in the winter. Her strategy was to avoid setting foot on the plantations, instead arranging to meet the escaping slaves eight to ten miles away. Most escapes took place on Saturday nights because the slaves wouldn't be missed until Monday and could therefore gain more ground. When slaveholders realized they were missing, they'd launch search parties and put up signs, which Tubman's hired help would quickly remove.

Those closest to Tubman claimed her faith in God was the source of her

strength. She believed that God is a deliverer and protector of the weak. As she guided the slaves north, Tubman said, she would listen intently for the voice of God, then proceed where He guided her. Thomas Garrett, a fellow abolitionist, said of Tubman, "I never met any person of any color who had more confidence in the voice of God."

Tubman's notorious efforts on behalf of slaves so enraged slaveholders that they posted a forty-thousand-dollar reward for her capture. But Tubman's motto and the philosophy that guided her mission was "I can't die but once." Despite the dangerous work she engaged in and the constant target on her back, she was never apprehended.

Following the Civil War, Tubman made her home in Auburn, New York. Although she received numerous awards, she spent her last years in poverty. Finally, thirty years after the war, she was granted a government pension for the work she did for the Federal Army.

I'm going to hold
steady on You. You've
got to see me through.

—HARRIET TUBMAN, RECITED
REGULARLY WHEN SHE LED RUNAWAY
SLAVES TO FREEDOM IN THE NORTH

WILLIAM TYNDALE

(1494–1536)

William Tyndale was an Oxford and Cambridge–educated scholar who strongly supported church reform. He moved to London in 1523 with the goal of translating the Bible into English. Such work was forbidden, but Tyndale believed, along with Martin Luther and other Protestant reformers, that the Scriptures should establish the doctrines and practices of the church and should therefore be available in the language of the people. His beliefs put him at odds with the Established Church of England.

In 1524, Tyndale relocated to Germany, a safer location to conduct his work, and sought the help of Martin Luther at Wittenberg to finish his translation. He completed his English translation of the New Testament in Cologne in 1525, and by 1526, just one year later, smuggled copies had already arrived in England.

The Roman Catholic Church denounced Tyndale's work and labeled him a heretic. Tyndale disappeared into hiding and began the task of translating

the Old Testament from Hebrew to English. Despite their efforts, King Henry VIII and Cardinal Thomas Wolsey's agents were unable to find Tyndale.

In 1534, Henry VIII split from the Catholic Church, marking the beginning of the English Reformation. At this point, Tyndale believed it was safe to come out of hiding. But shortly after he emerged, his friend Henry Phillips betrayed him. Tyndale was arrested for heresy and imprisoned for almost a year and a half in Vilvoorde Castle. In October 1536, he was put on trial and was convicted of both treason and heresy and sentenced to death. Tyndale was subsequently executed by strangulation and burned at the stake, but by then, thousands of copies of his New Testament translation were already in circulation.

Just before his death, Tyndale reportedly cried out, "Lord, open the king of England's eyes." That dying prayer was answered three years later, when King Henry VIII published the "Great Bible" (aka the Coverdale Bible), which was based on Tyndale's work. And his work has been the basis of every English translation since.

Lord, open
the king of
England's eyes.

—The alleged last words
of William Tyndale

GEORGE WASHINGTON

(1732–1799)

The first president of the United States was born at his family's plantation in the British colony of Virginia on February 22, 1732. Little is known about Washington's early education, but as a teenager, he showed an aptitude for mathematics, and he became a successful surveyor, which allowed him to earn enough money to begin to acquire land.

In December 1752, Washington was appointed as a commander of the Virginia militia, despite having no military experience. He was ultimately charged with leading all of Virginia's militia forces during the French and Indian War. After resigning from his commission, Washington was elected to the Virginia House of Burgesses, where he served until 1774.

By 1775, the American Revolutionary War had begun. Washington was chosen as commander in chief of the Continental Army. When the conflict ended, he was named a national hero.

On January 7, 1789, the first United States presidential election was

held, and Washington easily won. When he took office, the United States was a small country with only eleven states and a population of four million people, and there was no precedent for him to follow with regard to either domestic or foreign relations. Knowing that he would set the example for future presidents, Washington worked tirelessly to model integrity. He maintained cordial relations with other countries but preferred to remain neutral with regard to foreign conflicts.

In 1796, after two terms as president, Washington retired. In his final address, he pleaded that the new nation maintain the highest standards domestically and be minimally involved with foreign powers. The United States Senate still reads this address each February as they observe Washington's birthday.

I now make it my earnest prayer, that God would have you, and the State over which you preside, in His holy protection, that He would incline the hearts of the Citizens to cultivate a spirit of subordination and obedience to Government, to entertain a brotherly affection and love for one another, for their fellow Citizens of the United States at large, and particularly for their brethren who have served in the Field, and finally, that He would most graciously be pleased to dispose us all, to do Justice, to love mercy, and to demean ourselves with that Charity, humility, and pacific temper of mind, which were the Characteristics of the Divine Author of our blessed Religion, and without an humble imitation of whose example in these things, we can never hope to be a happy Nation.

—George Washington

JOHN WESLEY

(1703–1791)

———————————

John Wesley was born into the devout Anglican home of Samuel and Susanna Wesley. Wesley's father was a priest, and his mother taught religion to John and eighteen siblings.

When Wesley grew up, he attended Oxford, where he proved himself a competent scholar and was soon ordained as an Anglican minister. Later, he would admit that at the time of his ordination, he lacked saving faith. It was not until 1783, when Wesley attended a gathering at which someone read Martin Luther's preface to the book of Romans, that Wesley said his heart felt "strangely warmed." It was then that he trusted Christ alone for salvation.

Wesley was invited by fellow preacher George Whitefield to assist in his rapidly growing ministry, and Wesley soon became the new leader of the movement. However, Wesley was at odds with the tenets of Calvinism,

particularly the doctrine of predestination. Soon the two preachers went separate ways.

It was not Wesley's intention to found a new denomination, but as he and others began to meet in private homes and the spiritual fervor at the meetings grew, the Methodist denomination was born. He went on to preach an estimated forty thousand sermons during his ministry. By the time of his death, the Methodist denomination had expanded rapidly, and today there are more than thirty million Methodists across the globe.

Wesley became known for the saying, "Do all the good you can, by all the means you can, in all the ways you can, in all the places you can, at all the times you can, to all the people you can, as long as ever you can." That advice is as appropriate today as it was in Wesley's time.

I put myself wholly into Thy hands: put me to what Thou wilt, rank me with whom Thou wilt; put me to doing, put me to suffering, let me be employed for Thee, or laid aside for Thee, or trodden under foot for Thee; let me be full, let me be empty, let me have all things, let me have nothing, I freely, and heartily resign all to Thy pleasure and disposal.

—JOHN WESLEY

GEORGE WHITEFIELD

(1714–1770)

———————————————

George Whitefield was arguably the most well-known religious figure of the eighteenth century.

He was born and raised in Gloucester, England. Growing up, Whitefield was fond of theater, often skipping school to practice for his upcoming performances. Those early communication skills that he was honing would later become useful in his preaching.

Whitefield worked his way through Pembroke College, Oxford, by waiting on wealthier students. During that time, he met a group of Methodists who nicknamed themselves "the Holy Club." Brothers Charles and John Wesley led the group. In the company of his newfound friends, Whitefield experienced what he described as a new birth and resolved to become a Christian missionary. He began preaching around London and was surprised by the size of the crowds and the interest he drew. But Whitefield's

preaching was unlike anything the crowds had heard before, and he left them mesmerized.

In 1738, Whitefield embarked on a preaching trip that would take him to the colonies of America. His first stop was in Philadelphia, Pennsylvania, and even the largest churches could not accommodate the thousands of people who came to hear him preach, so he moved his meetings outdoors. Frequently when he preached, his audiences numbered more than the town's population.

Over the years, Whitefield's influence grew, and his impact was so great that in time he was labeled America's first cultural hero. It has been estimated that during his lifetime he preached at least eighteen thousand times to as many as ten million people.

God give me a deep
humility, a well-guided
zeal, a burning love,
and a single eye, and
then let men or devils
do their worst.

—George Whitefield

WILLIAM WILBERFORCE

(1759–1833)

William Wilberforce was born on August 24, 1759, in Hull (in the northern part of England), the son of a wealthy business owner. He attended Cambridge University, where he met his lifelong friend William Pitt the Younger, who would eventually become prime minister.

Wilberforce became a member of Parliament for Hull in 1780 and would later represent Yorkshire, the ceremonial county of which Hull is a part. After becoming an evangelical Christian, his interest shifted to social reform, and he was especially concerned with improving factory conditions in Britain.

The work of abolitionist Thomas Clarkson had an enormous influence on Wilberforce. Clarkson and others were working for an end to the slave trade in England. British ships were transporting slaves from Africa to the West Indies in wretched conditions, to be bought and sold as merchandise. Wilberforce readily agreed to lobby for the abolition of the slave trade,

and for eighteen years he consistently introduced anti-slavery motions in Parliament. The slave trade was abolished in 1807, but it didn't free those who were already slaves. That would not come for another quarter century.

In 1802, Wilberforce began working with the reformer Hannah More in the Association for the Better Observance of Sunday. The organization's goal was to provide children, regardless of race or economic status, with steady education in reading and religion and access to personal hygiene. He also played a pivotal role in encouraging Christians to serve as missionaries to India.

In 1825, Wilberforce retired from politics. He died eight years later, on July 29, 1833, shortly after the House of Commons passed the act that finally freed all slaves in the British Empire.

O Lord, do Thou vouchsafe Thy quickening Spirit; without Thee I can do nothing. Mortify in me all ambition, vanity, vain-glory, worldliness, pride, selfishness, and aversation from God, and fill me with love, peace, and all the fruits of the Spirit.

—William Wilberforce

DORA YU

(1873–1931)

———————————————

Dora Yu was a prominent twentieth-century Chinese evangelist and Bible teacher. She was born at the American Presbyterian Mission compound in 1873, where her father was training to be a minister.

At age fifteen, Dora Yu left home to attend medical school. During her first two years of study, both of her parents died. Despite her loss, she remained in medical school for eight years, during which time she made a personal decision for Christ. When she was twenty-three, she and another student became the first female graduates of the medical school. Soon she would heed the call to the mission field.

As early as 1897, Dora Yu traveled as a missionary to Korea, becoming one of China's first cross-cultural missionaries. There, she practiced medicine and shared the gospel with the local women. Her friend and mentor, Josephine Campbell, whom she had met in medical school, had become a maternal figure to her, and together they opened Barwha Girls' School and

Louisa Walker Chapel. Dora Yu remained in Korea until October 1903, when she returned to China.

The Chinese church was experiencing a time of growth, and in 1904, Dora Yu gave up practicing medicine to devote her life to full-time ministry. Seeing the growing needs of the church, she founded the Bible Study and Prayer House, which would eventually become the Jiangwan Bible School. In May 1909, Dora Yu published one of the earliest hymn books of the Chinese church titled *A Hymn Book for Revival and Evangelistic Meetings*.

Dora Yu continued to travel throughout the southern provinces of China, preaching at revivals. It is believed that Chinese church leader and author Watchman Nee became a Christ-follower after hearing Dora Yu preach the gospel.

Keep me living in the heavenly realm; keep me dead to sin and alive in God; give me a spirit of obedience and childlike compliance with God's will; possess my life and prompt me to take into account the needs of others; soak me with His love, so that I might be like God in my love toward others; help me see the things of this world from God's point of view and always watchfully await the return of the Lord of glory.

—DORA YU

BIBLIOGRAPHY

"18 Martin Luther Quotes That Still Ring True." *Relevant* magazine website, published October 31, 2017. https://relevantmagazine.com/god/18-martin-luther-quotes-still-ring-true.

"About Dr. King." The King Center website, accessed July 17, 2018. http://www.thekingcenter.org/about-dr-king.

"About Henri Nouwen." Henri Nouwen Society website, accessed July 17, 2018. https://henrinouwen.org/about/about-henri/.

"Abraham Lincoln." The White House website, accessed July 17, 2018. https://www.whitehouse.gov/about-the-white-house/presidents/abraham-lincoln/.

Allen, Richard. *The Life, Experience, and Gospel Labors of the Rt. Rev. Richard Allen*. (Philadelphia: F. Ford and M.A. Riply, 1880), 31. https://books.google.com/books?id=_lZGAAAAYAAJ.

Augustine. *Confessions: A New Translation by Sarah Ruden*. (New York: Modern Library, 2017), 25. https://books.google.com/books?id=JddLDwAAQBAJ.

Benjamin Franklin and Jonathan Edwards: Selections from Their Writings. Edited by Carl Van Doren. (New York: Charles Scribner's Sons, 1920), 251–252. https://books.google.com/books?id=5mIEAQAAIAAJ.

"Billy Graham Biography." Billy Graham Evangelistic Association website, accessed July 17, 2018. https://memorial.billygraham.org/biography/.

"Billy Graham, Evangelist to the World, Dead at Age 99." Billy Graham Evangelistic Association website, published February 21, 2018. https://billygraham.org/story/billy-graham-evangelist-to-the-world-dead-at-age-99/.

Bonhoeffer, Dietrich. "Prayers for Fellow Prisoners," *Letters and Papers from Prison*. Edited by Eberhard Bethge, translated by Reginald H. Fuller. (New York: The Macmillan Company, 1959), 67–68. https://archive.org/stream/DietrichBonhoefferLettersFromPrison/Dietrich_Bonhoeffer_Letters_from_Prison_djvu.txt.

Booth, Evangeline Cory. *The Song Book of the Salvation Army*, no. 830. https://hymnary.org/text/the_world_for_god_the_world_for_god.

Bounds, E. M. *E. M. Bounds on Prayer*. (New Kensington, UK: Whitaker House, 1997), 7–8, 341.

Calvin, Jean and John Calvin. *Steward of God's Covenant: Selected Writings*. Edited by John F. Thornton and Susan B. Varenne. (New York: Vintage Books, 2006), 332. https://books.google.com/books?id=sGHKcZI3XAMC.

Carter, Joe. "9 Things You Should Know About Elisabeth Elliot." The Gospel Coalition website, published June 15, 2015. https://www.thegospelcoalition.org/article/9-things-you-should-know-about-elisabeth-elliot/.

Celtic Christian Spirituality: An Anthology of Medieval and Modern Sources. Edited by Oliver Davies and Fiona Bowie. New York: Continual International Publishing Group, 1995.

Chambers, Oswald. *My Utmost for His Highest.* (Uhrichsville, OH: Barbour, 1935), May 22.

"Charles Spurgeon." *Christianity Today* website, accessed July 18, 2018. http://www.christianitytoday.com/history/people/pastorsandpreachers/charles-spurgeon.html.

"Corrie ten Boom Biography." Biography.com website, accessed July 16, 2018. https://www.biography.com/people/corrie-ten-boom-21358155.

Crosby, Fanny J. "Hear and Answer Prayer." Hymnary.org website, accessed July 16, 2018. https://hymnary.org/text/i_am_praying_blessed_savior.

"Dietrich Bonhoeffer: German Theologian and Resister." *Christianity Today* website, accessed July 16, 2018. http://www.christianitytoday.com/history/people/martyrs/dietrich-bonhoeffer.html.

Douglass, Frederick. *Narrative of the Life of Frederick Douglass.* (Cambridge, MA: The Belknap Press of Harvard University Press, 2009), 71–72. https://books.google.com/books?id=HnAktoctDuIC.

Du Bois, W. E. B. *Prayers for Dark People.* Edited by Herbert Aptheker. (Amherst, MA: The University of Massachusetts Press, 1980), 21. https://books.google.com/books?id=qtP3zFARAuEC.

"Frederick Douglass." PBS.org website, accessed July 16, 2018. https://www.history.com/topics/black-history/frederick-douglass.

Galli, Mark, and Ted Olsen. *131 Christians Everyone Should Know.* Nashville: B&H, 2000.

"George Washington." History.com website, accessed July 18, 2018. https://www.history.com/topics/us-presidents/george-washington.

"George Washington Carver Biography." Biography.com website, accessed July 16, 2018. https://www.biography.com/people/george-washington-carver-9240299.

George Washington Carver: In His Own Words. Edited by Gary R. Kremer. (Columbia: University of Missouri Press, 1987), 137. https://books.google.com/books?id=5q6eTEJb_ioC&pg.

Goyer, Tricia. *Prayers That Changed History.* (Grand Rapids, MI: Zonderkidz, 2015), 16, 21, 172.

Graham, Billy. "A Prayer for America by Billy Graham." National Day of Prayer website, accessed August 30, 2018. http://www.nationaldayofprayer.org/a_prayer_for_america_by_billy_graham.

Graves, Dan. "Evangeline Cory Booth Spent Her Years for God." Christianity.com website), last updated July, 2007. https://www.christianity.com/church/church-history/timeline/1901-2000/evangeline-cory-booth-spent-her-years-for-god-11630799.html.

Hawn, C. Michael. "History of Hymns: 'Precious Lord, Take My Hand.'" Discipleship.org website, accessed July 16, 2018. https://www.umcdiscipleship.org/resources/history-of-hymns-precious-lord-take-my-hand.

"Helen Keller Biography and Chronology." American Foundation for the Blind website, accessed July 17, 2018. http://www.afb.org/info/about-us/helen-keller/biography-and-chronology/123.

"Helen Keller's Education and Literary Career." American Foundation for the Blind website, accessed July 17, 2018. http://www.afb.org/info/about-us/helen-keller/biography-and-chronology/biography/1235#education.

Jackson, Charreah. "Borrow a Prayer from Oprah Winfrey, Maya Angelou and Other Powerful Women to Get You Through." *Essence* (blog), published December 1, 2017. https://www.essence.com/lifestyle/famous-prayers-oprah-winfrey-maya-angelou-other-powerful-women.

"John Newton." *Christianity Today* website, accessed August 31, 2018. https://www.christianitytoday.com/history/people/pastorsandpreachers/john-newton.html.

"J. S. Bach: Soli Deo Gloria—To the Glory of God Alone." Christianity.com website, published July 19, 2010. https://www.christianity.com/church/church-history/church-history-for-kids/j-s-bach-soli-deo-gloria-to-the-glory-of-god-alone-11635057.html.

Kempis, Thomas à. *The Imitation of Christ*. (Uhrichsville, OH: Barbour Publishing, 2013), 20. https://books.google.com/books?id=ueMXjXqYuyoC.

King Jr., Martin Luther. *Thou, Dear God: Prayers That Open Hearts and Spirits*. Edited by Lewis V. Bladwin. (Boston: Beacon Press, 2011), 147. https://books.google.com/books?id=oKyBy8Ti1hoC.

"Later Years and Death." Frederick Douglass Heritage website, accessed September 4, 2018. http://www.frederick-douglass-heritage.org/later-years-death/.

Lawson, Steven. "Theologian for the Ages: John Calvin." Ligonier Ministries blog, published October 9, 2017. https://www.ligonier.org/blog/theologian-ages-john-calvin/.

Lawson, Steven. "William Tyndale's Final Words." Ligonier Ministries blog, published February 18, 2015. https://www.ligonier.org/blog/william-tyndales-final-words/.

Lee, Jarena. *Religious Experience and Journal of Mrs. Jarena Lee*. (Philadelphia: Printed and Published for the Author, 1849), 10. https://books.google.com/books?id=hNASAAAAYAAJ.

Lewis, C. S. *The Pilgrim's Regress*. (Grand Rapids, MI: Wm. B. Eerdmans Publishing, 2014), 163.

Li, Yading. "Dora Yu." *Biographical Dictionary of Chinese Christianity* website, accessed July 17, 2018. http://bdcconline.net/en/stories/yu-dora.

"Lincoln's Second Inaugural Address." The National Museum of American History website, accessed August 31, 2018. http://americanhistory.si.edu/lincoln/election-1864.

"Lottie Moon." International Mission Board of the Southern Baptist Convention website, accessed July 17, 2018. https://www.imb.org/who-was-lottie-moon.

Luther's Prayers. Edited by Herbert. F. Brokering. (Minneapolis: Augsburg, 1994), 31.

"Martin Luther: Passionate Reformer." *Christianity Today* website, accessed July 17, 2018. http://www.christianitytoday.com/history/people/theologians/martin-luther.html.

"Mary McLeod Bethune." National Women's History Museum website, accessed July 16, 2018. https://www.womenshistory.org/education-resources/biographies/mary-mcleod-bethune.

McDaniel, Debbie. "10 Amazing Things You Never Knew about Corrie Ten Boom." Crosswalk.com website, published June 26, 2016. https://www.crosswalk.com/faith/women/10-amazing-things-you-never-knew-about-corrie-ten-boom.html.

McPherson, Aimee Semple. *This Is That: Personal Experiences, Sermons, and Writings of Aimee Semple McPherson, Evangelist*. (Los Angeles: Bridal Call Publishing House, 1919), 15. https://books.google.com/books?id=_oVDAAAAIAAJ.

Metaxas, Eric. *Bonhoeffer: Pastor, Martyr, Prophet, Spy*. (Nashville: Thomas Nelson, 2010), 360.

Metaxas, Eric. "The Test of Forgiveness: Corrie ten Boom." FaithGateway.com website, accessed August 29, 2018. https://www.faithgateway.com/forgiveness-corrie-ten-boom/#.W4WFGNOWy70.

Mikels, Juana. "Daily Prayer by Elisabeth Elliot." JuanaMikels.com blog, published October 2, 2013. http://www.juanamikels.com/2013/10/daily-prayer-by-elisabeth-elliot.html.

Moody, D. L., et al. *The Gospel Awakening*. (St. Louis, MO: Scammel & Co, 1878), 723–724. https://books.google.com/books?id=2XFBAQAAMAAJ.

"More Information about William Tyndale." BBC History website, accessed July 18, 2018. http://www.bbc.co.uk/history/people/william_tyndale/.

Mother Teresa. *In the Heart of the World: Thoughts, Stories, and Prayers*. Edited by Becky Benenate. (Novato, CA: New World Library, 1997), 105–106. https://books.google.com/books?id=l8iKoxjsvicC.

Mulhall, Thomas A. *A Lasting Prophetic Legacy: Martin Luther King Jr., the World Council of Churches, and the Global Crusade Against Racism and War*. (Eugene, OR: Wipf & Stock, 2014), 217–18.

Müller, George. *A Narrative of Some of the Lord's Dealings with George Müller*, Volume 1. (London, J. Nisbet & Co., 1855), 266. https://books.google.com/books?id=WhY9AAAAcAAJ.

Nicholls, Michael Kenneth. "Spurgeon's College." *Christianity Today*, Issue 29, 1991. https://www.christianitytoday.com/history/issues/issue-29/spurgeons-college.html.

Nouwen, Henri J.M. *With Open Hands*. (Notre Dame, IN: Ave Maria Press, 2006), 27. https://books.google.com/books?id=qkpQCwAAQBAJ.

"Obama's Favorite Theologian? A Short Course on Reinhold Niebuhr." Pew Research Center website, published May 4, 2009. http://www.pewforum.org/2009/05/04/obamas-favorite-theologian-a-short-course-on-reinhold-niebuhr/.

"Oswald Chambers: Preacher Who Gave His Utmost." *Christianity Today* website, accessed July 16, 2018. http://www.christianitytoday.com/history/people/innertravelers/oswald-chambers.html.

"Peace Prayer of Saint Francis." Loyola Press website, accessed July 16, 2018. https://www.loyolapress.com/our-catholic-faith/prayer/traditional-catholic-prayers/saints-prayers/peace-prayer-of-saint-francis.

Petry, Ann. *Harriet Tubman: Conductor on the Underground Railroad*. New York: Open Road Integrative Media, Inc., 2015.

Pierson, A. T. *George Müller of Bristol*. Peabody, MA: Hendrickson, 2008.

Platt, David. "Lottie Moon: The Long Shadow of a Tiny Missionary Giant." International Mission Board of the Southern Baptist Convention website, accessed August 31, 2019. https://www.imb.org/2018/07/23/lottie-moon-story/.

Reeves, Michael. "10 Things You Should Know about Charles Spurgeon." Crossway website, published February 19, 2018. https://www.crossway.org/articles/10-things-you-should-know-about-charles-spurgeon/.

"Rosa Parks." History.com website, accessed July 17, 2018. https://www.history.com/topics/black-history/rosa-parks.

Schlesinger, Jr. Arthur. "Forgetting Reinhold Niebuhr." *New York Times Sunday Book Review*, published

September 18, 2005. http://www.nytimes.com/2005/09/18/books/review/forgetting-reinhold
-niebuhr.html.

Spurgeon, Charles Haddon. *C. H. Spurgeon's Prayers: Prayers from Metropolitan Pulpit*. (New York: Fleming
H. Revell Company, 1906), 90–91. https://books.google.com/books?id=1P1DAAAAYAAJ.

Stowe, Harriet Beecher. *Religious Studies, Sketches, and Poems*. (Boston: Houghton, Mifflin, and
Company, 1896), 321.

The Communion of Saints: Prayers of the Famous. Edited by Horton Davies. Grand Rapids, MI: William B.
Eerdmans Publishing Company, 1990), 72.

The Essential Reinhold Niebuhr. Edited by Robert McAfee Brown. (New Haven, CT: Yale University Press,
1986), 251. https://books.google.com/books?id=eB6MyJk2fvQC.

The Faith of Helen Keller. Edited by Jack Belck. (Kansas City, MO: Hallmark Cards, Inc., 1967), 21. http:
//www.archive.org/stream/onfaithhelen/onfaithhelen_djvu.txt.

The Westminster Collection of Christian Prayers. Edited by Dorothy M. Stewart. (Louisville, KY:
Westminster John Knox Press, 1999), 121–123. https://books.google.com/books?id=kfvh5CkU6
-AC.

"This Far by Faith: Thomas Dorsey." PBS.org website, accessed July 16, 2018. http://www.pbs.org
/thisfarbyfaith/people/thomas_dorsey.html.

Truth, Sojourner. *The Narrative of Sojourner Truth*. (Los Angeles: Enhanced Media, 2017), 53–54. https:
//books.google.com/books?id=8WmVDgAAQBAJ.

United States Holocaust Memorial Museum (website). "Dietrich Bonhoeffer." *Holocaust Encyclopedia*
website, accessed July 16, 2018. https://www.ushmm.org/wlc/en/article.php?ModuleId=10008205.

"Upbringing & Studies." The King Center website, accessed July 17, 2018. http://www.thekingcenter.
org/upbringing-studies.

Washington, Eric. "Jarena Lee: Trailblazing African American Preacher and 'self-made' woman."
Christianity Today website, published May 23, 2017. https://www.christianitytoday.com
/history/2017/may/jarena-lee.html.

Washington, George. "From George Washington to the States, 8 June 1783." *Founders Online*, National
Archives website, last modified June 13, 2018. https://founders.archives.gov/documents
/Washington/99-01-02-11404.

Wesley, John. *Directions to Penitents and Believers, for Renewing Their Covenant with God*. (London: Printed
by Thomas Cordeux, 1816), 10. https://books.google.com/books?id=iEtVAAAAcAAJ.

White, Rev. Lisa Beth. History of Missiology. "Carmichael, Amy Beatrice (1867–1951)." Boston
University School of Theology website, accessed July 16, 2018. http://www.bu.edu/missiology
/missionary-biography/c-d/carmichael-amy-beatrice-1867-1951/.

Whitefield, George. *Letters of George Whitefield, for the Period 1734–1742*. (Carlisle, PA: Banner of Truth
Trust, 1976), 33. https://books.google.com/books?id=ooLZAAAAMAAJ.

Wilberforce, Robert Isaac and Samuel Wilberforce. *The Life of William Wilberforce*. (Philadelphia: Henry
Perkins, 1839), 255. https://books.google.com/books?id=EiZFsgJkqoMC.

"William Wilberforce (1759–1833)." BBC History website, accessed July 18, 2018. http://www.bbc
.co.uk/history/historic_figures/wilberforce_william.shtml.